The Ultimate Little FROZEN DRINKS BOOK

RAY FOLEY

sourcebooks

Published by Sourcebooks, Inc.
P.O. Box 4410, Naperville, Illinois 60567-4410
(630) 961-3900
Fax: (630) 961-2168
www.sourcebooks.com

Originally published in 2001

The Library of Congress has catalogued the second edition as follows:

Foley, Ray.
  Ultimate little frozen drinks book / Ray Foley.
    p. cm.
  Includes index.
  1. Cocktails. 2. Alcoholic beverages. 3. Blenders (Cookery). I. Title.
  TX951.F5949 2006
  641.8'74—dc22

                          2005025116

               Printed and bound in Canada.
               WC 10 9 8 7 6 5 4 3 2 1

This book is dedicated to all the blended
cocktail drinkers and bartenders who stir, shake,
and serve.
Also to Jaclyn Marie and Ryan Foley
and the rest of the tribe!

ACKNOWLEDGMENTS

Bacardi USA, Inc.
Barton Incorporated
Brown-Forman Beverages Worldwide
Coco Lopez, Inc.—Jose Suarez, R. Jake Jacobsen
Imperial Brands, Inc. (Sobieski Vodka)—Chester Brandes, Timo Sutinen, Carolina Merino
InterBev USA
International Beverage Company, Inc. (Angostura Rum)—Peter Schwartz, Dave Conroy
Jim Beam Brands Worldwide, Inc.
McCormick Distilling—Vic Morrison, Doc Sullivan
National Cherry Board—Cheryl Kroupa
Rémy Amerique
SKYY Spirits, LLC.—Gerry Ruvo
Vita-Mix Corporation—Rula Stamatis
Waring Products

Special thanks to Jimmy Zazzali, Laura Keegan, Matt Wojciak, John Cowan, Lauren Saccone, Michael Cammarano, and Marvin Solomon.

In addition, to all those who submitted recipes to www.bartender.com and the readers of *Bartender Magazine*.

All recipes have been alphabetized for your convenience.

Techniques of Mixing

1. Blend—All, yes all, cocktails are to be blended with ice. Therefore, all instructions may not read "blend" at the end of each recipe or include ice in the list of ingredients.

2. Glasses—You should use your imagination on choice of glassware. This will add your personal signature to each cocktail. Any type of drinking vessel is permitted. Let your creativity pour wild.

3. Ingredients—Please only use the BEST ingredients—the top of the line. You would not buy cheap meat when cooking a steak. Use top brands—they make top cocktails.

4. Have Fun!

All recipes with this icon have been submitted by one of America's top bartenders. Enjoy!

Publisher's Note: This book and the recipes contained herein are intended for those of a legal drinking age. Please drink responsibly and ensure that you and your guests have a designated driver when consuming alcoholic beverages.

Raw Egg Warning: Some recipes contained in this book call for the use of raw eggs. The Food and Drug Administration advises caution in consuming raw and lightly cooked eggs, due to the slight risk of salmonella or other food-borne illness. To reduce this risk, the FDA recommends that you use only fresh, clean, properly refrigerated and pasteurized eggs with intact shells. Always wash hands, cooking utensils, equipment, and work surfaces with warm, soapy water before and after they come in contact with eggs.

Short History of the Blender

Waring, universally known for introducing the first blender to American consumers, is one of today's leading manufacturers of professional-quality, small appliances for the home, food-service, and laboratory industries. The company was acquired on May 9, 1998, by Conair Corporation, which also owns Cuisinart.

Although the company is named after Fred Waring, a popular entertainer of the 1930s, 40s, and 50s, Waring did not actually invent the blender. He did, however, perfect the original version and introduce this version to retailers and consumers—which ultimately became a big success. Waring history has it that in 1936, Fred Waring had just finished a radio broadcast in New York's Vanderbilt Theater when Fred Osius, dressed in outlandish striped pants, a cutaway coat, and a bright lemon-yellow tie, approached the entertainer with his latest invention. Osius was looking for someone to finance a new mixer that would "revolutionize people's eating habits."

Waring was intrigued with the concept of a mixer such as the one Osius described, and he agreed to back the new product, even when the prototype failed to work the first time. Six months and $25,000 later, the prototype still didn't work. However, Waring remained enthusiastic and with his support the engineering and production problems were solved in time to introduce the new "Miracle Mixer" (as it was then called) at the National Restaurant Show in Chicago in 1937.

Thanks to Waring's own promotion of the blender on the radio and through a singing group aptly named "The Waring Blendors," the blender became a permanent fixture in restaurants and bars. It wasn't long before consumers decided that they needed blenders in their kitchens as well. Ultimately, department- and specialty-store sales increased, and the blender became a household appliance for home chefs.

World War II temporarily halted blender production, but in 1946, sales took off again as consumer demand grew. Product innovations continued, with the introduction of color-coordinated blenders and attachments that crushed ice and ground coffee. Solid-state controls were among the most significant product changes. In the 1950s, new uses for the blender were constantly emerging, including applications in research laboratories. In fact, Dr. Jonas Salk used a Waring blender with an Aseptic Dispersal Container attachment to develop his lifesaving polio vaccine.

During the late 1960s, design and engineering breakthroughs by Waring led to the creation of a more versatile blender that was more efficient and widely affordable. While maintaining its leadership in the blender market, Waring capitalized on its strong brand recognition and expanded its product line with a broad range of fine-quality kitchen appliances.

Fred Waring died in 1984, but his vision for a top-quality blender lives on as Waring continues to manufacture an innovative line of top-performance blenders for the home and for commercial use.

Hamilton Beach
Commercial Blender Tips

1. Make sure you purchase the right blender for your application.

   * Frozen drinks without alcohol require a blender with a more powerful motor.

* Determine the container size based on the maximum drink size and maximum number of drinks that will be blended at one time.

* Stainless steel vs. plastic container is a personal preference, but there's more "show" and ease of loading with plastic and better insulation with stainless steel.

* Blenders with timers allow other tasks to be performed while blending.

* Programmed cycle blenders provide optimum blend performance.

2. Use ice cubes that have fewer air pockets or a smaller cube size for ease in blending.

3. Add liquid ingredients first.

4. Measure ice with the glass the drink will be served in.

5. Ice should be added until it fills to the top of the liquid.

6. If ice cream is in the recipe, it should be added last.

7. Wait until the blade stops rotating before removing the lid.

8. Make sure the blender is off before removing or installing a container.

9. Check the clutch for wear, and replace as needed. (Removes easily per instruction card.)

10. Check the blade assembly periodically, and replace on a regular basis.

Vita-Mix's Top Ten Tips for Blending Liquids

1. Secure the container cover tightly before turning the blender on.

2. Do not place fingers or other objects, such as spoons or spatulas, in the blender container while the motor is running.

3. Do not remove the container cover while processing liquids.

4. If adding beer to a drink, stir it in last. Do not place beer in a blender and then turn it on.

5. When making ice cream drinks, in general, use soft ice cream and add it to the container last. With a Vita-Mix blender, however, you can add hard-packed ice cream or frozen yogurt at any point.

6. For single-serve drinks, add ice first. Pulse ice once or twice. Then add the wet ingredients.

7. When mixing drinks, switch to a higher speed if the motor seems to be laboring.

8. Always unplug the machine before cleaning it.

9. To clean a blender container, fill it halfway with water. Add a few drops of dishwashing detergent. Turn the motor on and blend for a few seconds. Empty the container and rinse it.

10. Keep the machine clean. Store it on a clean surface. Clean the vents regularly.

The History of Coco Lopez

Once upon a Time There Was No Piña Colada...

The heart of the coconut has long been an important ingredient of many delicious desserts in the tropical islands, but getting the coconut cream from the pulp was a task in itself.

Don Ramon

There had to be an easier way, and one man set out to find it. In his small laboratory in Puerto Rico in the 1950s, Don Ramon Lopez Irizarry developed the original Coco Lopez, a delicious homogenized cream made from the tender meat of sun-ripened Caribbean coconuts and blended with the exact proportion of natural cane sugar.

There is only one right moment and way to blend the basic ingredients that make up the original Coco Lopez cream of coconut. And this magical moment always took place in Don Ramon's kitchen.

Limited Production

Success came too suddenly for Don Ramon Lopez Irizarry. His production facilities were limited to his personal efforts. This is when Industrias La Famosa, Puerto Rico's largest processors of canned products, and Don Ramon agreed on mutual goals. The fusion became a transcendental success! After his agreement with Industrias La Famosa, he limited the secret of his expertise to be shared by only two of its stockholders. This unique product was granted with U.S. Patent #2426834.

Recipes Made Easy

Getting the cream from the coconut for desserts and other native dishes was a tedious and laborious task. Coco Lopez made it easy. For this reason it is preferred by homemakers and has earned its place in the kitchens of the best restaurants and hotels in Puerto Rico.

The Flavorful Piña Colada

Suddenly, Coco Lopez became the basis for a fabulous tropical drink called the Piña Colada (pronounced: pee-nyah coh-lah-dah). The date of the drink's first appearance is still under debate.

Quite a few bartenders and part-time mixers—including one at Barra China in Old San Juan (1963) and another at the Caribe Hilton Hotel in San Juan (1954)—have claimed to be the inventors of the "Official Beverage of Puerto Rico," as proclaimed by the tourism department of Puerto Rico. But there's no doubt that the unique combination of Coco Lopez cream of coconut, pineapple juice, and Puerto Rican rums turns out to be the most refreshing natural tropical cocktail you'll ever have. As a matter of fact, only the original Coco Lopez cream of coconut meets the necessary conditions of flavor and consistency to prepare the perfect piña colada.

Coco Lopez Piña Colada Goes International

Tourists who came to Puerto Rico and tasted a piña colada became true fans, and they took Coco Lopez back home so they could again enjoy "The Taste of the Tropics."

Today, Coco Lopez has expanded its distribution into more than fifty countries around the world. You can find it in Europe, the Middle East, Japan, Central and South America, the United States, and as close as your nearest supermarket.

Enjoy an Original.

Original Piña Colada

2 cups crushed ice
4 oz. Coco Lopez cream of coconut
4 oz. pineapple juice
2 oz. Puerto Rican rum
Maraschino cherry and pineapple wedge
   for garnish

Makes two servings.

Family Piña Colada

For a refreshing piña colada the whole family will enjoy, just leave out the rum.

All cocktails should be blended with ice.

A Day at the Beach

1 oz. Disaronno amaretto
1 oz. orange juice
½ oz. pineapple juice
Splash grenadine

Abbot's Delight

⅓ cup ice, crushed
¼ cup pineapple juice
2 oz. Frangelico
½ oz. small ripe banana, sliced
2 dashes Angostura bitters

Aberdeen Sour

1 ½ oz. Cutty Sark
1 oz. lemon juice
1 oz. orange juice
½ oz. Hiram Walker triple sec

Absolut Citron Colada

2 oz. Coco Lopez cream of coconut
2 oz. pineapple juice
1 ½ oz. Absolut Citron
1 oz. crème de banana
2 tbsp. lime juice
2 tbsp. superfine sugar
Coconut and pineapple slices for garnish

Absolut Kurant Freeze

1 fresh banana
1 ½ oz. Absolut Kurant
½ oz. crème de banana
3 fresh raspberries
2 tbsp. superfine sugar

Absolut Stress

1 oz. Absolut vodka
1 oz. cranberry juice
1 oz. pineapple juice
½ oz. Coco Lopez cream of coconut
½ oz. peach schnapps
Maraschino cherry for garnish

Acapulco Gold

1 ¼ oz. Jose Cuervo Especial tequila
1 oz. sweet and sour mix
½ oz. Grand Marnier

Agent Orange

2 oz. orange juice
1 oz. vodka
1 oz. Yukon Jack
½ oz. apple schnapps
½ oz. melon liqueur
¼ oz. grenadine

Aggravation

2 oz. cream
1 oz. Kahlúa
½ oz. scotch

Alaskan Blue Whale

1 ½ oz. gin
1 oz. blue Curaçao
1 oz. Coco Lopez cream of coconut

Albatross Sea Breeze

2 oz. fresh lime juice
1 ½ oz. Midori melon liqueur
1 oz. gin
1 egg white

Albino Eskimo

1 ½ oz. cream or milk
1 oz. Kahlúa
½ oz. amaretto
½ oz. strawberry schnapps
Strawberry for garnish

Alexander's Sister

3 oz. heavy cream
2 oz. gin
1 oz. white crème de menthe

Ali-Colada

2 oz. Alizé
2 oz. Coco Lopez cream of coconut
Dash Bacardi rum
Pineapple wedge for garnish

Alien Urine Sample

1 oz. sweet and sour mix
¾ oz. crème de banana
¾ oz. Malibu rum
¾ oz. peach schnapps
¼ oz. Midori melon liqueur
⅛ oz. blue Curaçao

Blend all ingredients except blue Curaçao. Pour into cocktail glass. Float blue Curaçao on top of cocktail.

Alizé Dreamsicle

2 oz. orange juice
2 oz. pineapple juice
1 ½ oz. Alizé
½ oz. Absolut vodka
½ oz. Coco Lopez cream of coconut
1 tbsp. Major Peters' grenadine

Almond Joy

2 oz. cream
1 oz. Hiram Walker amaretto
1 oz. Hiram Walker white crème de cacao

Aloha

2 oz. freshly squeezed orange juice
2 oz. pineapple juice
2 oz. vanilla ice cream
1 oz. Coco Lopez cream of coconut
1 oz. dark rum
½ oz. lime juice
Maraschino cherry and pineapple spear for
   garnish

Ambrosia Punch

1 20-oz. can crushed pineapple, undrained
1 15-oz. can Coco Lopez cream of coconut
2 cups apricot nectar, chilled
2 cups orange juice, chilled
1 ½ cups light rum
1 liter club soda, chilled

Puree the pineapple and cream of coconut in a blender until smooth. Combine the pureed mixture, nectar, juice, and rum in a punch bowl and mix well.

Add club soda just before serving, and serve over ice.

Makes 15–20 servings.

An Alternate Root

3 oz. orange juice
1 ½ oz. Hiram Walker Old Fashioned root beer schnapps

Angostura Sundae

2 oz. vanilla ice cream
1 oz. gold rum
½ tsp. Angostura bitters
Maraschino cherry for garnish

Aphrodite's Lover Potion

3 oz. pineapple juice
1 ½ oz. Metaxa brandy

Apple Daiquiri

1 oz. apple schnapps
1 oz. light rum
½ oz. sweet and sour mix
¼ peeled apple

Apple Graham Crispy

3 oz. vanilla ice cream
1 oz. apple schnapps
½ oz. brandy
½ oz. Irish cream
¼ cup graham cracker crumbs for garnish

Apple Hummer

1 ½ oz. DeKuyper apple barrel schnapps
1 oz. Gilbey's rum
1 oz. vanilla ice cream
Maraschino cherry for garnish

Appleton V/X Orange Daiquiri

Juice of 1 orange
1 oz. Appleton Estate V/X Jamaican rum
Juice of ¼ lime
1 tsp. superfine sugar
Slice of orange rind and a sprig of mint for
    garnish

Appleton V/X Piña Colada

2 oz. Appleton Estate V/X Jamaican rum
2 oz. pineapple juice
¾ oz. coconut cream
¾ oz. heavy cream
Maraschino cherry and pineapple spear for
    garnish

Apricot Colada

3 oz. Coco Lopez cream of coconut
2 oz. vanilla ice cream
1 ½ oz. Hiram Walker apricot brandy

Apricot Piña

1 ½ oz. light rum
1 ½ oz. pineapple juice
1 oz. Coco Lopez cream of coconut
½ oz. apricot brandy

Apricot Sunset

2 oz. Marie Brizard apricot liqueur
1 oz. cranberry juice
1 oz. lemon juice
1 oz. orange juice
Few drops gin

April Shower

3 oz. pink grapefruit juice, chilled
1 ½ oz. Bacardi Silver rum

Ariana's Dream

3 oz. orange juice
1 oz. Alizé
1 oz. crème de cacao
½ oz. Bacardi
Fresh strawberry for garnish

Bacardi Alexander

¾ oz. Bacardi light rum
½ oz. cream or 2 oz. vanilla ice cream,
    depending upon desired thickness
½ oz. dark crème de cacao
Grated nutmeg for garnish

Bacardi Amber Daiquiri

2 oz. Bacardi dark rum
2 tsp. fresh lime juice or lemon juice
½ tsp. superfine sugar
½ tsp. heavy cream
Grated nutmeg for garnish

Bacardi Banana Colada

½ ripe banana
1 ½ oz. Bacardi light or dark rum
1 oz. Coco Lopez cream of coconut
Banana wedge for garnish (optional)

Bacardi Banana Daiquiri

⅓ ripe banana
1 ½ tsp. Bacardi light rum
1 tsp. superfine sugar
½ tsp. lime juice or lemon juice

Bacardi Beachcomber

1 ½ oz. Bacardi light or dark rum
1 oz. lemon juice or lime juice
½ oz. cherry liqueur

Bacardi Big Apple

1 ½ oz. Bacardi light or dark rum
¾ oz. grenadine
¾ oz. lemon juice or lime juice
½ oz. apple brandy
Slice of apple for garnish (optional)

Bacardi Black Dirty Colada

2 oz. pineapple juice
1 ¼ oz. Bacardi black rum
1 oz. Coco Lopez cream of coconut

Bacardi Blossom

1 ¼ oz. Bacardi light rum
1 oz. orange juice
½ oz. lemon juice
½ tsp. superfine sugar

Bacardi Cocktail

1 ½ oz. Bacardi light rum
1 oz. lime juice
½ oz. grenadine
½ tsp. superfine sugar

Bacardi Daiquiri*

1 ½ oz. Bacardi light rum
½ oz. lime juice or lemon juice
½ tsp. superfine sugar

 *THE ORIGINAL DAIQUIRI WAS MADE WITH
BACARDI RUM IN 1896.

Bacardi Grasshopper

1 oz. Bacardi light rum
½ oz. heavy cream
¼ oz. green crème de menthe

Bacardi Hemingway

1 ½ oz. Bacardi light rum
Juice of ½ lime
¼ oz. grapefruit juice
¼ oz. maraschino liqueur

Bacardi Key Largo

2 oz. orange juice
1 ½ oz. Bacardi black rum
1 ½ oz. coconut cream
Maraschino cherry for garnish

Bacardi Orange Bowl

1 ½ oz. Bacardi light rum
1 oz. orange juice
1 oz. cream, milk, or half-and-half, depending
    upon desired thickness
Orange section for garnish (optional)

Bacardi Orange Daiquiri

1 ½ oz. Bacardi light rum
1 oz. orange juice
2 tsp. lime juice or lemon juice
1 tsp. superfine sugar

Bacardi Peach Daiquiri

2 oz. Bacardi light rum
1 oz. lime juice or lemon juice
2 tbsp. fresh, peeled peach halves
1 tsp. superfine sugar

Bacardi Piña Colada

2 oz. pineapple juice
1 ¼ oz. Bacardi light-dry or gold rum
1 oz. Coco Lopez cream of coconut

Bacardi Pineapple Daiquiri

2 oz. Bacardi light rum
½ slice canned pineapple
1 tbsp. lime juice
1 tsp. superfine sugar

Bacardi Rum Runner

1 ¼ oz. Bacardi dark rum
½ oz. blackberry brandy
½ oz. crème de banana
½ oz. lime juice
⅛ oz. grenadine

Bacardi Stinger

2 oz. Bacardi dark rum
1 oz. white crème de menthe

Bacardi Strawberry Daiquiri

½ cup fresh or frozen whole strawberries
2 oz. Bacardi light rum
1 tbsp. lime juice
1 tsp. superfine sugar
Whole strawberry for garnish

Bahama Mama

2 oz. apple juice
1 oz. orange juice
½ oz. Coco Lopez cream of coconut
½ oz. light rum
Dash Angostura grenadine
Dash triple sec

Baileys Alexander

½ oz. Baileys Irish cream
½ oz. cognac
½ oz. white crème de cacao

Baileys Banana Blaster

1 oz. Baileys Irish cream
1 oz. Malibu rum
½ oz. crème de banana or ½ ripe banana

Baileys Blizzard

3 oz. vanilla ice cream
1 oz. Baileys Irish cream
½ oz. brandy
½ oz. peppermint schnapps
Maraschino cherry for garnish

Baileys Blizzard II

1 oz. Baileys Irish cream
½ oz. Metaxa brandy
½ oz. Rumple Minze peppermint schnapps

Baileys Chill-Out Cappuccino

8 oz. double-strength coffee
1 ½ oz. Baileys Irish cream
½ oz. cream
2 tsp. superfine sugar
Whipped cream for garnish
Powdered cinnamon or cocoa powder for
  garnish

Baileys Coconut Frappe

2 oz. Baileys Irish cream
2 oz. milk
1 oz. Malibu rum
Toasted coconut for garnish

Baileys Cream Dream

2 oz. Baileys Irish cream
2 oz. half-and-half

Baileys Dream Shake

2 oz. Baileys Irish cream
2 oz. vanilla ice cream
Maraschino cherry for garnish

Baileys Float

3 oz. vanilla ice cream, softened
2 oz. Baileys Irish cream

Blend the Baileys Irish cream and 2 ½ oz. of the ice cream. Pour into glass and top with the remaining ice cream.

Baileys French Dream

2 oz. half-and-half
1 ½ oz. Baileys Irish cream
½ oz. raspberry liqueur

Baileys Frozen Mudslide

1 oz. Baileys Irish cream
1 oz. coffee liqueur
1 oz. Stolichnaya vodka

Baileys Iced Cappuccino

½ cup ice
3 oz. double-strength coffee, cooled to
    room temperature
2 oz. Baileys Irish cream
1 oz. half-and-half
2 tsp. superfine sugar

Baileys Italian Dream

2 oz. half-and-half
1 ½ oz. Baileys Irish cream
½ oz. Disaronno amaretto

Baileys Light Shake

4 oz. vanilla frozen yogurt
2 oz. Baileys Irish cream light

Baileys Malibu Slide

1 oz. Baileys Irish cream
1 oz. Kahlúa
1 oz. Malibu rum

Baileys Rum Yum

1 oz. Baileys Irish cream
1 oz. cream or milk
1 oz. Malibu rum
Maraschino cherry for garnish

Baileys Russian Dream

2 oz. half-and-half
1 ½ oz. Baileys Irish cream
½ oz. vodka

Bali Dream

1 oz. Coco Lopez cream of coconut
1 oz. orange juice
1 oz. white rum
½ oz. crème de banana
½ oz. dark rum
Splash grenadine

Ballsbridge Bracer

3 oz. orange juice
1 oz. Tullamore Dew
¾ oz. Irish Mist
1 egg white

Banana B. Jones

1 banana
1 ½ oz. crème de banana
1 oz. Coco Lopez cream of coconut
1 oz. vanilla ice cream
Whipped cream, banana slice, and
    maraschino cherry for garnish

Banana Banshee

1 ½ oz. crème de banana
1 oz. vanilla ice cream
½ oz. white crème de cacao

Banana Boat

1 ½ oz. tequila
1 oz. lime juice
½ oz. crème de banana

Banana Chi Chi

½ banana
2 oz. Coco Lopez cream of coconut
1 ½ oz. pineapple juice
1 ½ oz. vodka

Banana Colada

1 medium banana
2 oz. Coco Lopez cream of coconut
1 ½ oz. rum
1 tsp. lemon juice

Banana Cow

3 oz. milk
1 ½ oz. Puerto Rican rum
1 tbsp. banana, ripe
2 tsp. superfine sugar

Banana Cream Pie

½ ripe banana, peeled
1 oz. vanilla ice cream
1 oz. vodka
½ oz. crème de banana
½ oz. Irish cream

Banana Daiquiri

1 ½ oz. light rum
¼ banana, sliced
1 oz. crème de banana
½ oz. heavy cream
½ oz. lime juice
1 tsp. sugar or honey (optional)

Banana Daiquiribe

1 very ripe banana
2 oz. CocoRibe
½ oz. lime juice

Banana Di Amore

2 oz. orange juice
1 oz. amaretto
1 oz. sweet and sour mix
½ oz. crème de banana

Banana Frosted

2 oz. vanilla or banana ice cream
½ cup milk
½ ripe banana
1 oz. Disaronno amaretto

Banana Lemon Cooler

1 ½ oz. Bacardi light rum
¾ oz. lemon juice
¾ oz. pineapple juice
¼ ripe banana
½ oz. lemon soda for float

Blend everything but lemon soda. Float lemon
soda on top.

Banana Lopez

2 oz. Coco Lopez cream of coconut
1 medium banana
1 tsp. lemon juice

Banana Mama

2 oz. pineapple juice
1 ½ oz. light rum
1 oz. Coco Lopez cream of coconut
1 oz. crème de banana
1 oz. fresh or frozen strawberries
½ oz. dark rum

Banana Margarita

2 oz. DeKuyper crème de banana
1 oz. freshly squeezed lime juice
1 oz. Sauza tequila
½ oz. DeKuyper triple sec

Banana Punch Frappe

1 ½ oz. Bacardi light rum
¾ oz. orange juice
½ oz. crème de banana

Banana Rama

2 oz. half-and-half
1 oz. Kahlúa
½ oz. crème de almond
½ oz. crème de banana

Banana Split

2 oz. half-and-half
¼ oz. crème de almond
¼ oz. crème de banana
¼ oz. Kahlúa
Whipped cream, maraschino cherry, and/or
    a banana slice for garnish

Banana Tree

1 ½ oz. crème de banana
¼ oz. crème de almond
2 oz. half-and-half
Whipped cream, maraschino cherry, and/or
    a banana slice for garnish

Banilla Boat

4 oz. vanilla ice cream
1 oz. Drambuie
½ oz. Hiram Walker crème de banana

Banshee

1 whole ripe banana, peeled
1 oz. crème de banana
1 oz. vanilla ice cream
½ oz. white crème de cacao

Reserve two slices of banana for garnish. Blend
the remainder with the ice cream and cordials.

Barbados Cocktail

2 oz. Mount Gay rum
½ oz. Cointreau
½ oz. sweet and sour mix

Barbary Coast

½ oz. Beefeater dry gin
½ oz. Cutty Sark
½ oz. heavy cream
½ oz. Hiram Walker white crème de cacao

Bareback Rider

2 oz. Mandarine Napoleon
1 tsp. superfine sugar
Juice of ½ lime
Two maraschino cherries for garnish

Barefoot Boy with Bongo

1 ½ oz. Campari
1 oz. rye
½ oz. dry vermouth
Twist of lemon peel for garnish

Basic Daiquiri

2 oz. white rum
1 oz. lime juice
1 tbsp. superfine sugar

Batida Abaci

2 oz. cachaça or light rum
½ cup pineapple chunks

Bay Bomber

1 oz. cranberry juice
1 oz. orange juice
1 oz. pineapple juice
1 oz. sweet and sour mix
¼ oz. gin
¼ oz. rum
¼ oz. tequila
¼ oz. triple sec
¼ oz. vodka
Splash of 151-proof rum for float

Blend everything but the 151-proof rum. Float splash of rum on top.

Bayou Juice

1 oz. amaretto
1 oz. Coco Lopez cream of coconut
1 oz. cranberry juice
1 oz. pineapple juice
1 oz. rum

Beach Bum's Cooler

2 oz. vanilla ice cream
¼ ripe banana
1 ½ oz. Coco Lopez cream of coconut
1 ¼ oz. Irish cream
¾ oz. light rum
¼ oz. crème de banana
Maraschino cherry for garnish

Beach Party

1 ½ oz. Bacardi light or dark rum
1 oz. grenadine
1 oz. lemon or lime juice
1 oz. orange juice
1 oz. pineapple juice

Beachcomber

4 oz. orange juice
1 oz. Galliano
1 oz. half-and-half
1 oz. triple sec

Beachcomber's Golddust

1 ½ oz. light rum
1 oz. Coco Lopez cream of coconut
1 oz. lime juice
½ oz. triple sec
½ tsp. superfine sugar

Beachcomber's Special

1 ½ oz. Bacardi light rum
¾ oz. lemon juice or lime juice
½ oz. orange Curaçao
¼ tsp. superfine sugar (optional)

Beachside Coco Lopez

3 oz. Coco Lopez cream of coconut
2 oz. Coco Lopez strawberry daiquiri mix
1 ½ oz. Midori melon liqueur
1 oz. Bacardi light rum

Bean Stalk

4 oz. heavy cream
1 ¼ oz. Kahlúa
¾ oz. rum

Beaujolais Cocktail

3 oz. Beaujolais
¼ cup ice
1 oz. rainbow sherbet
5 red seedless grapes for garnish

Bee Bite Cocktail

2 oz. orange juice
1 oz. light rum
Juice of 2 limes
2 tsp. grenadine

Beefeater Blue Devil

1 oz. Beefeater dry gin
¼ oz. lemon juice
Dash Hiram Walker blue Curaçao
Dash maraschino liqueur
½ tsp. powdered sugar

Bellini 2000

2 oz. peach schnapps
2 oz. sparkling wine
1 oz. Cruzan pineapple rum
1 tbsp. Coco Lopez cream of coconut
1 tbsp. Alizé for float

Blend everything but the Alizé. Float Alizé on top.

Bermuda Triangle

2 oz. cranberry juice
2 oz. orange juice
1 ½ oz. Gosling's Black Seal rum

Berry-Cherry Cream

3 oz. vanilla ice cream
1 ½ oz. chocolate cherry liqueur
1 ½ oz. crème de cassis
Maraschino cherry for garnish

Big Apple

3 oz. apple juice
2 oz. apple brandy
½ oz. amaretto
1 tbsp. applesauce
Ground cinnamon for garnish

Big Blue Sky

2 oz. pineapple juice
½ oz. blue Curaçao
½ oz. Coco Lopez cream of coconut
½ oz. light rum

Bikini

1 oz. orange juice
1 oz. peach nectar
1 oz. vodka
½ oz. peach schnapps
Splash lemon juice
1 oz. champagne, chilled

Blend first five ingredients, then add champagne.

Bikini Daiquiri

2 oz. Coco Lopez cream of coconut
1 oz. lime juice
¾ oz. Cruzan banana rum
¾ oz. Cruzan pineapple rum

Bishop Cocktail

1 ½ oz. Bacardi light or dark rum
¾ oz. lemon or lime juice
¾ oz. red wine
1 tsp. superfine sugar (optional)

Bit O' Honey

2 oz. vanilla ice cream
1 oz. Baileys Irish cream
1 oz. white crème de menthe
Maraschino cherry for garnish

Black Forest

1 oz. chocolate ice cream
1 oz. vodka
½ oz. Chambord
½ oz. coffee liqueur
Shaved chocolate or sprinkles for garnish

Black Rose

½ cup fresh or frozen strawberries
1 ½ oz. cream or milk
½ oz. Chambord
½ oz. gold tequila
½ oz. Kahlúa

Black Rum Runner

3 oz. Coco Lopez rum runner mix
2 oz. Bacardi black rum

Black Seal Rum Runner

1 ¼ oz. Gosling's Black Seal rum
1 oz. crème de banana
¾ oz. blackberry liqueur
¾ oz. grenadine
½ oz. lime juice

Blackberry Cream

4 oz. cream
1 ½ oz. Hiram Walker blackberry brandy

Blackthorn

1 ½ oz. dry vermouth
1 ½ oz. Irish whiskey
3-4 dashes Angostura bitters
3-4 dashes Pernod

Sloe gin can be used in place of Irish whiskey.

Blizzard

1 ½ oz. bourbon
1 ½ oz. cranberry juice
½ oz. grenadine
½ oz. lime juice
1 tsp. superfine sugar

Bloodhound

2 oz. gin
1 oz. dry vermouth
1 oz. sweet vermouth
3 fresh strawberry halves

Blue Bayou

3 oz. sweet and sour mix
1 oz. Malibu rum
½ oz. blue Curaçao
½ oz. DeKuyper blueberry schnapps

Blue Gillati

½ oz. blue Curaçao
½ oz. DeKuyper blueberry schnapps
½ oz. Midori melon liqueur
½ oz. sweet and sour mix
½ oz. vodka

Blue Hawaiian

3 oz. pineapple juice
2 oz. Coco Lopez cream of coconut
1 ½ oz. light rum
1 oz. blue Curaçao

Blue Hawaiian II

4 oz. pineapple juice
1 ½ oz. Malibu rum
½ oz. blue Curaçao
Splash sweet and sour mix

Blue Heaven

1 oz. Hiram Walker blue Curaçao
1 oz. light rum
1 oz. pineapple juice
1 tsp. Coco Lopez cream of coconut

Blue Margarita

1 ½ oz. tequila
1 oz. lime juice or juice of ½ lime
½ oz. blue Curaçao
1 tsp. triple sec
Coarse salt for rim
Lime wedge for garnish

Blue Moon Margarita

2 oz. 100% silver agave tequila
2 oz. sweet and sour mix
1 oz. blue Curaçao
¼ oz. Grand Marnier
⅛ oz. Rose's sweetened lime juice
Lime wedge for garnish

Blue Sky

8 oz. pineapple juice
1 ½ oz. Canadian Mist
¾ oz. Bacardi light rum
¾ oz. blue Curaçao
Orange slice and maraschino cherry for
    garnish

Blue Tail Butterfly

3 oz. vanilla ice cream
1 oz. blue Curaçao
1 oz. white crème de cacao

Blue Whale

1 oz. Coco Lopez cream of coconut
1 oz. gin
¾ oz. Curaçao

Blueberries and Cream

2 oz. Coco Lopez cream of coconut
1 ½ oz. blueberry schnapps
½ oz. heavy cream

Blueberry & Cream

1 ½ oz. DeKuyper blueberry schnapps
1 oz. heavy cream or half-and-half

Blueberry Daiquiri

½ cup blueberries
2 oz. Bacardi light rum
1 oz. blueberry schnapps
1 oz. lemon or lime juice

Blushin' Russian

3 oz. vanilla ice cream
1 oz. Kahlúa
¾ oz. vodka
Splash of grenadine

Blushing Bride Cocktail

2 oz. Romana sambuca
1 oz. sloe gin

Boarsenberry

1 ½ oz. Gordon's wildberry vodka
1 oz. half-and-half, cream, or vanilla
    ice cream, depending upon desired
    thickness
¾ oz. Chambord
½ oz. Frangelico
¼ oz. crème de noyaux
4 blackberries and ground nutmeg for
    garnish

Bobby Buttercream

3 oz. butter pecan ice cream
3 oz. Southern Comfort
¼ tsp. Vermont maple syrup

Bossa Nova

3 oz. passion fruit juice
2 oz. dark rum
1 ½ oz. Galliano
1 oz. apricot brandy

Boston Breeze

3 oz. cranberry juice cocktail
1 ¼ oz. rum
1 oz. Coco Lopez cream of coconut

Boston Flip

1 oz. bourbon
1 oz. Madeira wine
1 egg yolk
½ tsp. Vermont maple syrup

Boston Southside

1 ½ oz. gin
1 ½ oz. sweet and sour mix
½ oz. lime juice
½ tsp. superfine sugar

Bourbon Slush

2 oz. sweetened tea
1 ½ oz. bourbon
1 oz. lemonade
½ oz. orange juice

Bow Street Special

1 ½ oz. Tullamore Dew
1 oz. lemon juice
½ oz. Hiram Walker triple sec

Brandied Peaches & Cream

1 ½ oz. Coco Lopez cream of coconut
1 oz. peach schnapps
1 oz. vanilla ice cream
¾ oz. brandy
Maraschino cherry for garnish

Brandy and Rum

2 oz. brandy
1 ½ oz. light rum
1 egg yolk
1 tbsp. lemon juice
1 tsp. superfine sugar

Brandy Bracer

2 oz. brandy
1 egg
1 tsp. lemon juice
1 tsp. superfine sugar
2 dashes Angostura bitters
2 dashes anisette

Brandy Cobbler

2 oz. brandy
1 tsp. blue Curaçao or triple sec
½ tsp. superfine sugar

Brandy Collins

2 oz. brandy
1 tsp. superfine sugar
½ lemon, peeled

Brandy Daisy

2 oz. brandy
1 tsp. grenadine
Juice of ½ lemon
Splash of club soda

Blend first three ingredients and top with club soda.

Brandy Egg Nog

2 oz. milk
1 whole egg
1 oz. brandy
1 oz. Jamaican rum
1 tsp. superfine sugar

Brandy Ice

2 oz. vanilla ice cream
1 ½ oz. brandy
½ oz. white crème de cacao
Maraschino cherry for garnish

Brown Bomber

2 oz. half-and-half or heavy cream
1 oz. DeKuyper crème de cacao
1 oz. DeKuyper root beer schnapps

Brown Cow

3 oz. vanilla ice cream
1 ½ oz. root beer schnapps
Root beer to fill

Brown Derby

1 ½ oz. Bacardi dark rum
¾ oz. lemon juice or lime juice
1 tsp. maple syrup

Brunswick Sour

1 ½ oz. Bacardi light rum
¾ oz. lime juice
½ tsp. superfine sugar
Claret wine for float

Blend everything but the Claret wine. Float Claret wine on top.

Bugsy's Baccio

2 oz. vanilla ice cream
1 oz. cranberry juice
¾ oz. Disaronno amaretto
½ oz. crème de cacao
½ oz. Malibu rum
3 mini Lazzaroni Amaretti cookies for
 garnish

Bull Fighter

2 oz. pineapple juice
1 ½ oz. Sauza Hornitos tequila
1 oz. Rose's lime juice
½ oz. grenadine

Bulldog Cocktail

1 ½ oz. Bacardi light or dark rum
¾ oz. lime juice
½ oz. cherry brandy
Maraschino cherry for garnish

Bumble Bee Stinger

1 oz. Rémy Martin cognac
¾ oz. Galliano
½ oz. Pernod

Bunny Bonanza

2 oz. gold tequila
1 oz. apple brandy
½ oz. lemon juice
¾ tsp. maple syrup
3 dashes triple sec
Lemon slice for garnish

Burnt Almond

1 oz. Kahlúa
1 oz. vanilla ice cream
1 oz. vodka
½ oz. amaretto

Bushwacker

2 oz. Coco Lopez cream of coconut
2 oz. half-and-half
2 oz. Kahlúa
½ oz. Bacardi black rum
½ oz. Hiram Walker dark crème de cacao

Busted Cherry

2 oz. cherry juice
1 oz. light rum
½ oz. amaretto
½ oz. dark crème de cacao
3 maraschino cherries for garnish
Whipped cream for garnish

Garnish with whipped cream and 3 maraschino
cherries in a hurricane glass.

 JERRY WOOD • PHOENIX, AZ

Butterfly Milk Punch

3 oz. milk
2 oz. cognac
1 oz. crème de cacao
½ tsp. superfine sugar
Dash Angostura bitters

Cacao Mint

3 oz. vanilla ice cream
1 oz. Hiram Walker spearmint schnapps
1 oz. Hiram Walker white crème de cacao
Maraschino cherry for garnish

Cactus Colada

2 oz. Coco Lopez cream of coconut
1 ¼ oz. tequila
1 oz. orange juice
1 oz. pineapple juice
¾ oz. Midori melon liqueur
½ oz. grenadine

California Coastline

2 oz. pineapple juice
1 oz. Malibu rum
1 oz. peach schnapps
½ oz. blue Curaçao
Pineapple slice for garnish

California Fizz

4 oz. orange juice
1 ½ oz. Bacardi light or dark rum
1 egg

Calm Voyage

1 oz. Bacardi light or gold rum
1 oz. orange juice
¼ oz. Hiram Walker apple brandy
Dash Angostura bitters

Calypso Cool-Aid

1 ¼ oz. Rhum Barbancourt
1 oz. pineapple juice
½ oz. lemon juice or lime juice
¼ tsp. superfine sugar
Club soda to fill
Pineapple spear and lime wheel for garnish

Calypso Daiquiri

1 ripe banana
1 ½ oz. Myers's Jamaican rum
1 ½ oz. sweet and sour mix
½ oz. half-and-half
1 tsp. vanilla extract
Mango slice for garnish

Calypso Highway

2 oz. Coco Lopez cream of coconut
2 oz. orange juice
2 oz. pineapple juice
1 oz. light rum
½ oz. blue Curaçao
½ oz. crème de banana

Camino Real

1 ½ oz. Gran Centenario Plata or
   reposado tequila
1 oz. orange juice
½ oz. crème de banana
Dash coconut milk
Dash lime juice
Lime slice for garnish

Candy

2 oz. orange sherbet
1 oz. Galliano
1 oz. Rémy Martin cognac
Dash maraschino liqueur
Chocolate chips or chocolate curls for garnish

Canyon Quake

2 oz. light cream
¾ oz. brandy
¾ oz. Irish cream
½ oz. amaretto
Maraschino cherry for garnish

Cape Colada

1 oz. Coco Lopez cream of coconut
1 oz. cranberry juice
1 oz. sweet and sour mix
1 oz. vodka
½ oz. peach schnapps

Captain Caribbean

3 oz. Kahlúa
1 ½ oz. coconut rum
Splash Galliano
Pineapple, orange, and banana slices for
    garnish

Captain Morgan Planter's Punch

3 oz. orange juice
1 ¼ oz. Captain Morgan spiced rum
½ oz. lemon or lime juice
1 tsp. superfine sugar
Dash grenadine

Captain Morgan Spiced Rum Daiquiri

1 ¼ oz. Captain Morgan spiced rum
Juice of ½ lime
1 tsp. superfine sugar

Captain Morgan Spiced Rum Piña Colada

2 oz. pineapple juice
1 oz. Coco Lopez cream of coconut
¼ oz. Captain Morgan spiced rum

Captain Morgan's Fruit Daiquiri

1 ¼ oz. Captain Morgan spiced rum
Juice of ½ lime
1 tsp. superfine sugar
5 large strawberries, ½ ripe banana,
    ½ peeled peach, or 4 oz. sliced, canned
    pineapple

Captain Morgan's Spyglass

2 oz. vanilla ice cream
1 oz. Captain Morgan spiced rum
1 tbsp. honey
Dash milk (optional)

Captain's Berry Daiquiri

½ cup strawberries or raspberries
1 ¼ oz. Captain Morgan spiced rum
1 tsp. lime juice
½ tsp. superfine sugar

Blend all ingredients, reserving one berry for garnish.

Captain's Colada

3 oz. pineapple juice
1 ¼ oz. Captain Morgan spiced rum
1 oz. Coco Lopez cream of coconut
Pineapple spear and maraschino cherry for
   garnish

Captain's Cream Delight

2 oz. orange juice
1 ¼ oz. Captain Morgan spiced rum
1 oz. Coco Lopez cream of coconut

Captain's Daiquiri

1 ¼ oz. Captain Morgan spiced rum
2 tsp. lime juice
½ tsp. superfine sugar
Lime wedge for garnish

Captain's Morgarita

3 oz. frozen limeade
1 oz. Captain Morgan spiced rum
½ oz. triple sec

Captain's Parrot

4 oz. pineapple juice
2 oz. orange juice
1 ½ oz. Captain Morgan spiced rum
1 oz. Parrot Bay
1 tbsp. maraschino cherry juice for float
Maraschino cherries for garnish

Blend everything but the maraschino cherry juice. Float cherry juice on top and garnish with cherries.

 ROBERT R. TOWSON • NEWARK, DE

Carabinieri

2 ¾ oz. orange juice
1 oz. tequila
1 egg yolk
¾ oz. Galliano
¼ oz. lemon juice

Cardinal's Cocktail

1 ½ oz. Bacardi light rum
1 oz. lime juice
¼ oz. grenadine
¼ oz. orgeat syrup
¼ oz. triple sec

Caribbean Colada

4 oz. pineapple juice
1 ½ oz. Rhum Grandier
1 ½ oz. Coco Lopez cream of coconut
Pineapple spear for garnish

Caribbean Cruise

3 oz. pineapple juice
2 oz. Coco Lopez cream of coconut
1 oz. coffee liqueur
1 oz. half-and-half
1 oz. dark rum

Caribbean Frost

4 oz. Coco Lopez cream of coconut
1 ½ oz. vodka (flavored vodka can be used)

Caribbean Grasshopper

1 ½ oz. Coco Lopez cream of coconut
1 oz. white crème de cacao
½ oz. green crème de menthe

Caribbean Gridlock

½ cup raspberries
2 oz. sweet and sour mix
½ oz. Bacardi light rum
½ oz. Cruzan Estate Diamond rum
½ oz. Grand Marnier
½ oz. Mount Gay Eclipse rum
1 oz. Chambord

Serve the shot of Chambord on the side.

Caribbean Joy

1 ½ oz. Bacardi light rum
1 oz. pineapple juice
¾ oz. lemon juice

Caribbean Passion

1 oz. pineapple juice
¾ oz. Passoã
½ oz. Mount Gay rum
Splash orange juice

Caribbean Queen

3 oz. Coco Lopez cream of coconut
2 oz. orange juice
1 ¼ oz. Bacardi Limon
½ oz. Cointreau

Caribbean Queen II

2 oz. lemonade
2 oz. orange juice
1 ½ oz. watermelon schnapps
1 oz. Coco Lopez cream of coconut
¼ oz. triple sec

Caribbean Romance

3 oz. Bacardi Superior white rum
2 pieces papaya
2 pieces banana
1 ½ oz. sugar syrup
1 oz. Coco Lopez cream of coconut
1 oz. lime juice
Orange slice, pineapple spear, and
    maraschino cherry for garnish

Caribbean Sunset

2 ½ oz. Bacardi
2 ½ oz. strawberry concentrate
1 ½ oz. carrot juice
1 ½ oz. Coco Lopez cream of coconut
1 ½ oz. coconut water
1 ½ oz. mango puree
Mango and cherry/palm tree stir stick for
    garnish

Caribbean Welcome

1 ½ oz. Bacardi light rum
1 oz. apricot brandy
1 oz. Coco Lopez cream of coconut
1 oz. pineapple juice
Maraschino cherry for garnish

Carousel

2 oz. gin
2 oz. Mandarine Napoleon
1 oz. lemon juice

Cassie's Delight

2 oz. Baileys Irish cream
1 ½ oz. Kahlúa
1 oz. milk
½ oz. crème de cacao

Catalina Margarita

4 oz. sweet and sour mix
1 ¼ oz. Jose Cuervo gold tequila
1 oz. blue Curaçao
1 oz. peach schnapps

Catherine Was Great!

2 oz. orange juice
1 oz. Stoli Strasberi vodka
½ oz. Disaronno amaretto
½ oz. light rum
1 tsp. triple sec

Cavalier

1 ½ oz. orange juice
1 ½ oz. Sauza tequila
⅓ oz. Galliano
½ oz. heavy cream
Maraschino cherry for garnish

CC Cider

3 oz. apple cider
1 oz. Canadian Club
½ oz. Hiram Walker cinnamon schnapps
¼ unpeeled red apple

Celtic Crush

2 oz. Celtic Crossing liqueur
2 oz. orange juice

Chambord Colada

2 oz. pineapple juice
1 ½ oz. Bacardi rum
1 ½ oz. Chambord
½ oz. Coco Lopez cream of coconut

Chambord Frost

1 ½ oz. Chambord
Juice of ½ lemon

Chambord Margarita

3 oz. margarita mix
1 oz. gold tequila
½ oz. Chambord
½ oz. triple sec

Chamborlada

3 oz. pineapple juice
2 oz. Coco Lopez cream of coconut
1 oz. Chambord
½ oz. Bacardi light rum
½ oz. Bacardi dark rum

Cherry Alexander

¾ oz. crème de cacao
¾ oz. premium brandy
½ oz. cherry brandy or cherry juice
6 maraschino cherries
¼ oz. half-and-half
Shaved chocolate or chocolate curls and a
    maraschino cherry for garnish

Serve in a brandy snifter.

 HEIDI EPLING • SEATTLE, WA

Cherry Amaretto Freeze

4 oz. vanilla ice cream
2 oz. amaretto
10 maraschino cherries

 MICHAEL MANGANARO • METAIRIE, LA

Cherry Amore

2 oz. vanilla ice cream
1 oz. cherry heering
½ oz. amaretto
½ oz. vodka
4 maraschino cherries and whipped cream
   for garnish

 LES HEMINGWAY • CINCINNATI, OH

Cherry Blossom

2 oz. sloe gin
1 oz. orange juice
1 tbsp. lemon juice
1 tbsp. maraschino cherry juice or cherry
   liqueur
Maraschino cherry for garnish

Cherry Bombe

1 oz. Dr. McGillicuddy's vanilla schnapps
1 oz. cherry juice
1 oz. cream
1 oz. Stoli Vanil
3 maraschino cherries for garnish

Serve in a tall glass. Make a cherry tree for garnish by taking one large drink straw and sticking cherries in stem first, so they hang over the edge.

 DUKE MOSAKOWSKI, 1999 MARASCHINO CHERRY CONTEST WINNER • NEW HARTFORD, NY

Cherry Bomber

1 oz. orange juice
½ oz. blackberry brandy
½ oz. Captain Morgan spiced rum
½ oz. cherry juice
½ oz. crème de banana
½ oz. Malibu rum
½ oz. Myers's rum
3 maraschino cherries for blending, plus
    2 for garnish
Bacardi 151 for garnish

Blend first seven ingredients and three cherries with ice. Fill two straws with Bacardi 151. Load remaining two cherries, stem down, in straws and enjoy.

Cherry Buster

½ oz. amaretto
½ oz. Tequila Rose
½ oz. white crème de cacao
3 maraschino cherries
Splash maraschino cherry juice

 CHRISTINE MERCKLE • IDAHO FALLS, ID

Cherry Buster II

1 ½ oz. cherry pucker
1 oz. orange juice
1 oz. vodka
Orange slice and maraschino cherry for
   garnish

Serve in a tall Tom Collins glass. Wrap the
orange slice around the maraschino cherry for
garnish.

 ROGER MALONEY • APPLETON, WI

Cherry Cheesecake A

1 part amaretto
1 part cream
1 part vanilla vodka
3 maraschino cherries

 D. ZIMMERMAN • DULUTH, MN

Cherry Cheesecake B

1 ½ oz. Dr. McGillicuddy's vanilla
1 oz. cherry juice

Cherry Cheesecake with Chocolate

3 oz. vanilla ice cream
1 oz. cherry brandy
1 oz. light crème de cacao
1 oz. softened cream cheese
Splash of milk
2 diced maraschino cherries, stems
   removed
Cherry juice
Chocolate syrup
Whipped cream and 2 whole maraschino
   cherries for garnish

Pour cherry juice and chocolate syrup into a poco grande glass. Top with a pyramid of whipped cream, two straws, and two stemmed cherries.

 JAY A. WELLE • MOORHEAD, MN

Cherry Cream

1 oz. Bacardi light rum
1 oz. cherry liqueur
1 oz. cream

Cherry Daiquiri

2 oz. prepared limeade
1 ½ oz. light rum
1 oz. maraschino cherry juice
½ oz. superfine sugar
4-8 maraschino cherries
Maraschino cherry for garnish

Cherry Fish

½ oz. ice
1 oz. light rum
½ oz. Rose's lime juice
7 Swedish Fish (a gelatin candy)
3 maraschino cherries for garnish

 MICHAEL ARNOLD • NEWPORT, RI

Cherry Flip

6 oz. Danish cherry wine
1 egg
2 tsp. superfine sugar
1 tbsp. lemon juice

Cherry Flurry

2 oz. vanilla ice cream
1 ½ oz. milk
1 oz. cherry juice
¾ oz. amaretto
½ oz. white crème de cacao
4 maraschino cherries for garnish

 NANCY WHITE • TEXARKANA, TX

Cherry Love

2 oz. vanilla ice cream
1 ⅓ oz. Bacardi light
½ oz. Cointreau
5 oz. maraschino cherries, plus one for
   garnish
Slice of lime for garnish

Pour all ingredients into a blender with a little ice. Serve in a margarita glass. Garnish with a slice of lime and a maraschino cherry in center; place on top of the drink to create a flower.

 ALBERTO MEZA, 1999 MARASCHINO CHERRY
CONTEST WINNER • SEATTLE, WA

Cherry Passion Potion

1 ½ oz. cherry juice
1 ½ oz. passion fruit juice
1 oz. white rum
Maraschino cherry dipped in dark
    chocolate for garnish

Blend and serve in a rocks glass.

 DOLORES LONG, 1999 MARASCHINO CHERRY
CONTEST WINNER • VAN NUYS, CA

Cherry Piña

1 ½ oz. light rum
1 ½ oz. pineapple juice
1 oz. Coco Lopez cream of coconut
½ oz. maraschino cherry juice
6 stemless, pitted maraschino cherries

Cherry Pop

1 oz. Malibu rum
½ oz. peach schnapps
Splash orange juice
5 maraschino cherries
Splash maraschino cherry juice
Whipped cream and a maraschino cherry
    for garnish

MARK LANGELL, 1999 MARASCHINO CHERRY
CONTEST WINNER • STATEN ISLAND, NY

Cherry Repair Kit

1 oz. amaretto
½ oz. crème de cacao
½ oz. half-and-half
½ oz. maraschino cherry juice
3 maraschino cherries

Blend all.

Cherry Ripe

2 oz. gin
1 oz. cherry brandy
1 oz. Kirsch

Chevoney

2 oz. vanilla ice cream
1 oz. Galliano
½ oz. Grand Marnier
½ oz. vodka

 NORBERT F. KARCH • BAILEYS HARBOR, WI

Chi Chi

1 ½ oz. Absolut vodka
1 ½ oz. Coco Lopez cream of coconut
¾ oz. pineapple juice

Chicago Style

¾ oz. Bacardi light rum
¼ oz. Hiram Walker anisette
¼ oz. Hiram Walker triple sec
¼ oz. lemon juice or lime juice

Chip Shot

1 oz. Irish cream
1 oz. Kahlúa
½ oz. half-and-half

Chiquita

¼ cup sliced banana
1 ½ oz. vodka
½ oz. crème de banana
½ oz. lime juice
1 tsp. orgeat syrup

Chiquita Punch

1 oz. crème de banana
¾ oz. heavy cream
¾ oz. orange juice
1 tsp. grenadine
Maraschino cherry for garnish

Chocolada

1 cup ice
2 oz. Bacardi light
1 ½ oz. crème de coconut
1 ½ oz. milk
1 oz. dark crème de cacao
Whipped cream and chocolate chips for
   garnish

Chocolate Almond Cream

2 oz. amaretto
1 oz. vanilla ice cream
½ oz. crème de cacao

Chocolate Almond Kiss

2 oz. vanilla ice cream
1 oz. Frangelico
½ oz. Absolut vodka
½ oz. dark crème de cacao

Chocolate Black Russian

2 oz. chocolate ice cream
1 oz. Kahlúa
½ oz. vodka

Chocolate Cherry Bomb

1 ½ oz. Godiva or Mozart chocolate liqueur
1 oz. half-and-half
Cherry juice and maraschino cherry for
    garnish

Blend with ice. Pour into a martini glass. Make
a pool of cherry juice in the center and add
maraschino cherry.

 STEVEN LASSOFF • SAN FRANCISCO, CA

Chocolate Cherry Chip Cocktail

2 oz. chocolate-chip ice cream
1 oz. cherry brandy
1 oz. maraschino cherry juice
½ oz. dark crème de cacao
¼ oz. amaretto
¼ oz. Kahlúa
Powdered cocoa, maraschino cherry, chocolate
   chips, and confectioners' sugar for garnish

Blend with chocolate-chip ice cream and dust
with cocoa. Garnish with chocolate cherry bombs.

Chocolate Cherry Bombs: Soak a maraschino
cherry in crème de cacao. Slit the cherry, stuff with
chocolate chips, and dip in confectioners' sugar.

 JEFF MARKLAND & SANDI BAJORSKI •
KENNEBUNKPORT, ME

Chocolate Colada

1 cup ice
2 oz. Coco Lopez cream of coconut
2 oz. half-and-half
2 oz. rum
1 oz. chocolate syrup

Chocolate Covered Strawberry

10 oz. strawberries
1 oz. rum
½ oz. Kahlúa
½ oz. triple sec

Chocolate Cream

1 oz. cream
¾ oz. Bacardi gold rum
¼ oz. Hiram Walker dark crème de cacao
¼ oz. Hiram Walker white crème de menthe

Chocolate Cream Dream

1 ½-2 oz. vanilla ice cream, depending
    upon desired thickness
1 oz. Irish cream liqueur
1 oz. Vandermint liqueur
½ oz. Du Bouchett butterscotch schnapps
    liqueur

Chocolate Kiss

¾ oz. Hiram Walker spearmint schnapps
¾ oz. Hiram Walker Swiss chocolate
    almond
¾ oz. Hiram Walker white crème de cacao

Chocolate Snow Bear

3 oz. chocolate ice cream
1 oz. amaretto
1 oz. dark crème de cacao
⅛ oz. chocolate syrup

Christmas Cranberry

1 ½ oz. Finlandia cranberry vodka
1 ½ oz. pineapple juice
1 oz. Coco Lopez cream of coconut
6–10 pitted and stemless maraschino cherries

Cider Nectar

3 oz. apple cider
1 tsp. brandy
1 tsp. lemon juice
1 tsp. superfine sugar

Citron Neon

1 ½ oz. Absolut Citron
1 oz. sweet and sour mix
½ oz. blue Curaçao
½ oz. Midori melon liqueur
Splash lime juice

Citrus Mist Colada

4 ½ oz. piña colada mix
1 ½ oz. Canadian Mist
2 oz. lemon-lime soda to fill
Maraschino cherry and lime slice for garnish

Citrus Supreme

2 cups lime- or lemon-flavored water
1 12-oz. can frozen lemonade
2 shots Gordon's citrus vodka
1 shot triple sec
Slice of lemon for garnish

Clover Cooler

4 oz. pineapple juice
½ oz. Baileys Irish cream
½ oz. blue Curaçao
½ oz. Malibu rum

Cockpit Cocktail

1 oz. Appleton gold Jamaican rum
½ oz. crème de cacao
½ oz. white crème de menthe
1 tbsp. heavy cream
1 tsp. Appleton white rum

Coco Amadine

2 oz. almond liqueur
1 oz. Coco Lopez cream of coconut

Coco Colada

4 oz. pineapple juice
1 ½ oz. Coco Lopez cream of coconut
1 ⅛ oz. dark crème de cacao
Pineapple spear and maraschino cherry for
   garnish

Coco Dream

½ cup ice
2 oz. vanilla ice cream
1 ½ oz. Coco Lopez cream of coconut
1 ½ oz. white crème de cacao

 COURTESY OF BENNIGAN'S RESTAURANTS, INC.

Coco Java

2 oz. coffee liqueur
1 oz. Coco Lopez cream of coconut

Coco Loco (Crazy Coconut)

3 oz. pineapple juice
2 oz. Coco Lopez cream of coconut
1 ½ oz. tequila
Pineapple spear and maraschino cherry for
    garnish

Coco Lopez Limonade

3 oz. Coco Lopez lemonade mix
1 oz. Bacardi Limón

Coco Lopez Limon Madness

1 oz. cranberry juice
1 oz. orange juice
½ oz. Bacardi Limón
½ oz. Coco Lopez cream of coconut

Coco Lopez Purple Passion

3 oz. Coco Lopez Purple Passion colada mix
1 ½ oz. Bacardi light rum

Cocobana

1 banana
2 oz. Bacardi light
1 oz. Coco Lopez Real Cream of Coconut

 SUSAN MCGOWAN • ODDFELLOWS RESTAURANT

Coco-Mocha Alexander

3 oz. Coco Lopez cream of coconut
2 oz. cold, black coffee
1 ½ oz. Irish Cream liqueur

Coco-Motion

4 oz. Coco Lopez cream of coconut
2 oz. lime juice
1 ½ oz. dark rum

Coconut Banana Colada

3 oz. pineapple juice
2 oz. Coco Lopez cream of coconut
2 oz. Cruzan coconut rum
¾ oz. Cruzan banana rum

Coconut Bellini

2 oz. Coco Lopez cream of coconut
2 oz. peach puree
½ oz. peach schnapps
3 oz. champagne

Blend first three ingredients. Top with champagne.

Coconut Bon Bon

2 oz. Coco Lopez cream of coconut
2 oz. vodka
1 oz. half-and-half
1 oz. Vandermint liqueur
Maraschino cherry for garnish

Coconut Colada

4 oz. Coco Lopez cream of coconut
2 oz. Malibu rum
2 oz. orange juice
1 oz. half-and-half

Coconut Daiquiri

1 ½ oz. Coco Lopez cream of coconut
1 ½ oz. rum
½ oz. lime juice

Coconut Grove

2 oz. Coco Lopez cream of coconut
1 oz. orange juice
1 oz. rum

Coconut Honey

2 oz. Coco Lopez cream of coconut
1 oz. dark rum
1 oz. honey

Coconut Punch

2 oz. Coco Lopez cream of coconut
1 ¼ oz. Bacardi light rum
3-4 tbsp. vanilla ice cream
¼ oz. lemon juice
Maraschino cherry for garnish

Coconut Punch II

2 oz. Coco Lopez cream of coconut
1 ¼ oz. Bacardi light rum
½ oz. lemon juice

Coconut Vodka Daiquiri
or Chi Chi

2 oz. Coco Lopez cream of coconut
2 oz. pineapple juice
1 oz. Finlandia vodka
½ oz. lime juice

Coffee Colada Freeze

2 oz. pineapple juice
1 oz. Coco Lopez cream of coconut
1 oz. Kahlúa
½ oz. rum

Coffee with Kirsch Cocktail
(Café Au Kirsch)

2 oz. Kirsch (or 1 oz. Kirsch, 1 oz. cognac)
2 oz. strong, cold coffee
1 egg white
1 ½ tsp. superfine sugar

Cointreau Colada

2 oz. Coco Lopez cream of coconut
2 oz. Cointreau
2 oz. pineapple juice

Cointreau Orange Freeze

3 oz. vanilla ice cream
2 oz. Cointreau
2 oz. orange soda to fill
Orange slice for garnish

Cointreau Santa Fe Margarita

2 oz. cranberry juice
2 oz. sweet and sour mix
1 ½ oz. Jose Cuervo gold tequila
¾ oz. Cointreau

Cointreau Strawberry Margarita

3 oz. frozen strawberries
2 oz. sweet and sour mix
1 ¼ oz. Jose Cuervo gold tequila
¾ oz. Cointreau

Cointreau-Band

2 oz. chocolate ice cream
2 oz. Cointreau
Maraschino cherry for garnish

Cold Orgasm

¾ oz. Absolut vodka
¾ oz. Baileys Irish cream
¾ oz. Kahlúa
Maraschino cherry for garnish

Colonel's Collins

1 oz. Cointreau
1 oz. gin
½ lime, peeled
Orange slice and maraschino cherry for
   garnish

Colorado Bulldog

4 oz. half-and-half
1 ¼ oz. Kahlúa
Cola to fill

Columbia Cocktail

1 ½ oz. Bacardi light or dark rum
1 oz. lemon juice
1 oz. raspberry syrup or several fresh or
    frozen raspberries

Comfort Colada

2 oz. pineapple juice
1 ½ oz. Southern Comfort
1 oz. Coco Lopez cream of coconut
Maraschino cherry for garnish

Comfortable Freeze

2 oz. pineapple juice
1 oz. Southern Comfort
½ oz. grenadine
Maraschino cherry for garnish

Comfortable Watermelon

1 ½ oz. Southern Comfort
1 oz. cranberry juice
1 oz. pineapple juice
½ oz. melon liqueur
½ oz. vodka

Comrade Coconut

3 oz. Coco Lopez cream of coconut
1 oz. vodka
½ oz. white crème de cacao

Continental

1 oz. Bacardi light rum
¾ oz. Rose's lime juice
¼ oz. green crème de menthe
¼ tsp. superfine sugar (optional)

Continental Stinger

1 ½ oz. vodka
¾ oz. Hiram Walker peppermint schnapps

Cool Banana

½ ripe banana
1 oz. lime juice
¾ oz. light rum
¾ oz. Romana sambuca
1 tsp. honey

Cool Irish Coffee Colada

1 ½ oz. Coco Lopez cream of coconut
1 oz. coffee liqueur
1 oz. heavy cream
1 oz. Irish whiskey

Cool Operator

2 oz. grapefruit juice
2 oz. orange juice
¾ oz. Midori melon liqueur
¼ oz. rum
¼ oz. vodka
Splash lime juice

Cool Southern Breeze

2 oz. Southern Comfort
1 oz. cranberry juice
1 oz. grapefruit juice
½ oz. crème de banana
Dash grenadine

Cooler

1 ½ oz. Bacardi light rum
¾ oz. lemon or lime juice
¼–½ oz. white crème de menthe
Sprig of mint for garnish

Coral Cocktail

1 ½ oz. Bacardi light rum
½ oz. apricot brandy
½ oz. grapefruit juice
½ oz. lemon juice or lime juice

Corn Popper Highball

2 oz. bourbon
1 oz. cream
1 egg white
1 tsp. grenadine

Cote Ce Cote La

1 ½ oz. Bacardi white rum
1 ½ oz. Coco Lopez cream of coconut
¼ oz. fresh banana
½ oz. grenadine
Orange slices and pineapple skin for garnish

Serve with a fancy straw.

Cotton Picker Cocktail

1 oz. lemon juice
1 oz. orange juice
1 oz. rum
1 oz. Southern Comfort

Cowboy's Punch

2 oz. Bacardi light or dark rum
1 oz. grapefruit juice
1 oz. lemon juice or lime juice
1 oz. pineapple juice

Coww Woww

1 ½ oz. Bacardi light or dark rum
1 oz. heavy cream
1 oz. lemon juice or lime juice

Cranberry Gin Sour

2 oz. gin
2 oz. light cream
1 oz. lemon juice or juice of ½ lemon
1 oz. lime juice or juice of ½ lime
½ oz. triple sec
1 tsp. superfine sugar
Club soda to fill
Cranberry juice to fill

Blend first six ingredients and top with cranberry juice and club soda.

Cream de la CocoRibe

1 cup vanilla ice cream
½ cup CocoRibe
2 slices canned pineapple, drained

Cream Puff

1 ½ oz. Bacardi light rum
2 oz. cream
½ oz. crème de noyaux (or almond liqueur)
1 egg white

Creamsicle Colada

2 oz. Bacardi spice
2 oz. pineapple juice
1 oz. Coco Lopez cream of coconut
½ oz. triple sec
½ oz. white crème de menthe
Orange and pineapple wedges for garnish

 JEANNINE CASE • ODDFELLOWS RESTAURANT

Creamy Grasshopper

2 oz. vanilla ice cream
1 oz. white crème de cacao
½ oz. green crème de menthe
Maraschino cherry for garnish

Creamy Screwdriver

6 oz. freshly squeezed orange juice
2 oz. vodka
1 egg yolk
½ tsp. superfine sugar

Crème de Café

1 oz. bourbon
1 oz. cold water
1 oz. instant coffee
1 oz. vanilla ice cream
Maraschino cherry for garnish

Cricket

1 oz. cream
¾ oz. Bacardi light rum
¼ oz. green crème de menthe
¼ oz. white crème de cacao
Maraschino cherry for garnish

Cruzan Frost

1 ½ oz. Cruzan white rum
½ oz. lemon sherbet
¼ oz. white crème de menthe
Mint sprig for garnish

Cuarenta y Tres Colada

2 oz. pineapple juice
1 oz. Coco Lopez cream of coconut
1 oz. Licor 43
½ oz. dark rum

Cuervo Acapulco Fizz

2 oz. orange juice
1 ½ oz. heavy cream
1 ½ oz. Jose Cuervo gold tequila
3 ice cubes
2 tsp. granulated sugar
2 dashes orange bitters
1 whole egg
Orange slice for garnish

Cuervo Alexander

2 oz. vanilla ice cream
1 oz. coffee liqueur
1 oz. Jose Cuervo gold tequila
1 oz. wild cherry brandy
Maraschino cherry for garnish

Cuervo Gold Margarita

2 oz. lime juice
2 oz. sweet and sour mix
1 ½ oz. Jose Cuervo gold tequila
1 oz. triple sec

Cuervo Raspberry Margarita

½ cup ice
½ cup raspberries, frozen
1 ½ oz. Jose Cuervo gold tequila
1 oz. lime juice
1 oz. triple sec
Raspberries for garnish

Cuervo Santa Fe Maggie

2 oz. cranberry juice
2 oz. sweet and sour mix
1 ¼ oz. Jose Cuervo gold tequila
½ oz. triple sec

Cuervo Strawberry Margarita

½ cup frozen strawberries
1 ½ oz. Jose Cuervo gold tequila
1 oz. lime juice
1 oz. triple sec

Czar Mandarine

1 ½ oz. cream
1 ½ oz. Mandarine Napoleon
1 ½ oz. vodka
Dash grenadine
Orange slice for garnish

Czarina

1 oz. Baileys Irish cream
1 oz. half-and-half or light cream
1 oz. Stoli Razberi vodka
1 tsp. maraschino liqueur

Mix all the ingredients except the maraschino liqueur. Drip maraschino liqueur on top.

Daiquabu

1 ½ oz. Malibu rum
½ oz. lime juice
¼ oz. fruit of your choice

Daiquiri

2 oz. lemon juice or lime juice
1 ½ oz. Canadian whisky
½ oz. light rum
½ oz. triple sec or Cointreau

Dark Canadian Colada

2 oz. heavy cream
1 ½ oz. Canadian whiskey
1 oz. Coco Lopez cream of coconut
½ oz. dark crème de cacao

Dark Mango Colada

3 oz. Coco Lopez mango mix
1 oz. Bacardi dark rum

Death by Chocolate

1 oz. vanilla ice cream
1 oz. vodka
½ oz. Baileys Irish cream
½ oz. dark crème de cacao

Deja Vu

1 cup ice
2 ½ oz. orange juice
1 ¼ oz. orange liqueur
1 oz. Coco Lopez cream of coconut
¼ oz. orgeat syrup

De-Minted De-Light

2 oz. lime juice
1 ¼ oz. Smirnoff vodka
½ oz. Sugar in the Raw
½ oz. triple sec
10 small mint leaves

Derby Daiquiri

1 oz. orange juice
1 oz. rum
½ oz. Cointreau
Splash lime juice

Desert Cooler

1 ½ oz. gin
1 oz. orange juice
½ oz. grenadine
½ oz. wild cherry brandy

Devil's Tail

1 ½ oz. light rum
1 oz. vodka
½ oz. lime juice
2 tsp. apricot brandy
2 tsp. grenadine

Dirty Colada

2 oz. pineapple juice
1 ½ oz. Bacardi black rum
1 oz. Coco Lopez cream of coconut
Maraschino cherry for garnish

Dirty Mutha

3 oz. chocolate ice cream
1 oz. coffee liqueur
½ oz. vodka
Maraschino cherry for garnish

Disarita Margarita

3 oz. margarita mix
1 oz. Jose Cuervo 1800 tequila
½ oz. Disaronno amaretto
Slice of lime for garnish

Disaronno Dreamsicle

2 oz. heavy cream
2 oz. orange juice
1 ½ oz. Disaronno amaretto
Maraschino cherry for garnish

Disaronno Shortcake

3 oz. cream
2 oz. strawberries
1 oz. Disaronno amaretto
1 oz. Tuaca
Maraschino cherry for garnish

Disaronno Smoothie

4–5 large strawberries
2 oz. Disaronno amaretto
1 oz. sour mix
Maraschino cherry for garnish

Dixieland Special

1 cup watermelon chunks, seedless
2 oz. vodka
Juice of ½ lime

Double Berry Coco Punch

20 oz. frozen strawberries in syrup, thawed
15 oz. Coco Lopez cream of coconut
48 oz. cranberry juice cocktail, chilled
16 oz. light rum (optional)
1 liter club soda, chilled

Puree the strawberries and cream of coconut in a blender until smooth. Combine the pureed mixture, cranberry juice, and rum (if desired) in a large punch bowl. Just before serving, add club soda and serve over ice.

Makes 18-20 servings.

Dr. Root

4 oz. sweet and sour mix
1 ½ oz. DeKuyper root beer schnapps
1 oz. Gilbey's light rum

Dreamsicle

1 part Cointreau
1 part heavy cream
1 part orange juice
Dash grenadine
Maraschino cherry for garnish

Dubonnet Fizz

2 oz. Dubonnet
Juice of ½ lemon
Juice of ½ orange
1 tsp. cherry brandy

Dubonnet Sour

2 oz. sweet and sour mix
1 oz. Dubonnet Rouge

Dynamic 'Rita

2 oz. orange juice
1 ¼ oz. Cuervo 1800 tequila
¾ oz. Grand Marnier
¼ oz. Rose's sweetened lime juice
Slice of lime for garnish

Dyn-O-Mite Daiquiri

3 oz. Marie Brizard orange banana liqueur
2 oz. rum
1 oz. lime juice
½ oz. triple sec

Egg Nog

2 qt. eggnog
8 oz. Vandermint liqueur
1 tbsp. grated nutmeg
1 tbsp. vanilla extract
Cinnamon sticks for garnish

Egg Sour

2 oz. brandy
1 egg
1 tsp. Cointreau
½ oz. lemon juice

Eggnog Dot

5 oz. milk or milk and cream
1 oz. rum, brandy, whiskey, or sherry
1 egg
1 tsp. superfine sugar

El Dorado

3 oz. orange juice
1 oz. Galliano
½ oz. white crème de cacao

Electric Lemonade

2 oz. sweet and sour mix
1 ¼ oz. vodka
½ oz. blue Curaçao
Splash 7-Up
Lemon slice for garnish

Electric Peach

1 oz. vodka
½ oz. cranberry juice cocktail
¼ oz. orange juice
¼ oz. peach schnapps
Lemon slice for garnish

Emerald Isle

2 oz. vanilla ice cream
¾ oz. Tullamore Dew
¾ oz. green crème de menthe
Maraschino cherry for garnish

Estate '85

2 oz. lemon sherbet
1 oz. Galliano
1 oz. Mount Gay light rum
Sprig of mint and wheel of kiwi for garnish

Eve's Apple

1 cup crushed ice
1 cup vanilla ice cream
1 ½ oz. apple juice
1 oz. apple-infused vodka
⅓ oz. Angostura lime juice
⅓ oz. blue Curaçao
¼ oz. Hot Damn! cinnamon schnapps

Garnish with a small orchid.

Eve's Temptation

1 cup ice
2 oz. apple juice
1 ¼ oz. vodka
1 oz. Coco Lopez cream of coconut
Ground cinnamon for garnish

Evita Cocktail

1 ½ oz. orange juice
1 oz. Midori melon liqueur
1 oz. Suntory vodka
½ oz. sweet and sour mix

Eye Opener

1 ½ oz. Bacardi light rum
½ oz. anisette
¼ oz. orange Curaçao
¼ oz. white crème de cacao
1 egg yolk

Falling Leaves

4 oz. orange juice
1 oz. Gosling's Black Seal rum
½ oz. Marie Brizard raspberry liqueur
Dash grenadine

Fern Gully

1 ½ oz. Bacardi light rum
1 oz. lemon juice or lime juice
1 oz. orange juice
¾ oz. Coco Lopez cream of coconut
¼ oz. orgeat syrup

Finlandia Cranberry Cooler

2 oz. Chambord
2 oz. cranberry juice
2 oz. Finlandia cranberry

Finlandia Sea Goddess

2 oz. Finlandia Classic
1 oz. Alizé Passion liqueur
Splash blue Curaçao

Fireman's Sour

1 ½ oz. Bacardi light rum
1 ½ oz. lemon juice or lime juice
¼ oz. grenadine
½ tsp. superfine sugar
Club soda to fill
Maraschino cherry and a lemon or lime
    wheel for garnish

First Cherry

3 oz. maraschino cherry juice
1 oz. cream
½ oz. Bacardi 151
½ oz. Baileys Irish cream
½ oz. cherry brandy
2 maraschino cherries for garnish

 CHERYL THORN • DUARTE, CA

Flamingo

2 oz. pineapple juice
1 oz. Beefeater dry gin
1 oz. Coco Lopez cream of coconut
1 oz. Major Peters' sweet and sour mix

Florida Banana

1 medium banana
4 oz. orange juice
2 oz. Coco Lopez cream of coconut
1 ¼ oz. vodka

Floridita

1 ½ oz. Bacardi light rum
1 oz. orange juice
½ oz. triple sec

Fluffy Duck

1 oz. advocaat
1 oz. gin
1 oz. orange juice
½ oz. Cointreau
Club soda to fill
Slice of orange and maraschino cherry for
    garnish

Flying Grasshopper

1 oz. vanilla ice cream
1 oz. vodka
¾ oz. green crème de menthe
¾ oz. white crème de cacao

Flying Kangaroo

1 ½ oz. pineapple juice
1 oz. Mount Gay rum
1 oz. vodka
¾ oz. Coco Lopez cream of coconut
¾ oz. orange juice
¼ oz. cream
¼ oz. Galliano

Foamy Orange Lime Cocktail

½ cup white port
2 tbsp. lime juice
½ oz. orange juice
1 tbsp. superfine sugar
1 egg white

Forbidden Fruit

3 oz. passion fruit juice
2 oz. Bacardi Select rum
2 oz. Coco Lopez cream of coconut
½ oz. shaved coconut
1 oz. Bacardi dark rum for float
Maraschino cherry for garnish

Blend first three ingredients. Wet the rim of a tulip or hurricane glass and dip it in the shaved coconut until the entire rim is covered. Fill with blended mixture, float the Bacardi dark rum on top, and garnish with cherry.

Forbidden Fruit II

1 oz. sweet and sour mix
1 oz. vodka
½ oz. Bacardi
⅛ oz. maraschino cherry juice
¼ oz. 151-proof rum for float
Maraschino cherry for garnish

Blend everything but the 151-proof rum. Float rum on top and garnish with cherry.

 LAURA HANKINS • REDDING, CA

Forbidden Jungle

1 ½ oz. pineapple juice
1 ½ oz. rum
1 oz. Coco Lopez cream of coconut
½ oz. peach schnapps
¼ oz. lime juice
Dash grenadine

Foreign Affair

1 oz. Metaxa brandy
½ oz. Romana sambuca
Juice of 1 lime

Forever Cherry

4 oz. cherry juice
1 ½ oz. Tropico rum
½ oz. cream
½ oz. Malibu rum
5 maraschino cherries
Maraschino cherry for garnish

 JIMM RAMUNND • PAINESVILLE, OH

Frangelico Freeze

4 oz. vanilla ice cream
1 ½ oz. Frangelico
Maraschino cherry for garnish

Freddie Fudpucker Freeze

4 oz. orange juice
1 ½ oz. tequila
¼ oz. Galliano

French Colada

1 ½ oz. pineapple juice
1 ½ oz. Puerto Rican white rum
1 oz. crushed ice
¾ oz. Coco Lopez cream of coconut
¾ oz. cognac
¾ oz. heavy cream
Splash crème de cassis

French Daiquiri

1 ½ oz. Bacardi light rum
¾ oz. lemon or lime juice
½ oz. Grand Marnier

French Dream

4 oz. ice
2 oz. half-and-half
1 ½ oz. Carolans Irish cream
½ oz. Chambord
Maraschino cherry for garnish

French Nipple

1 oz. amaretto
1 oz. Kahlúa
1 oz. vanilla ice cream
1 oz. vodka
Maraschino cherry for garnish

French Passion

3 oz. orange juice
2 oz. Passoã
½ oz. Rémy Martin cognac
Half slice of orange for garnish

Serve in a hurricane glass.

 BABE LOFFREDO • JERSEY CITY, NJ

French Roulette

3 oz. grapefruit juice
1 ½ oz. vodka
½ oz. Mandarine Napoleon
Lime slice for garnish

Frezsa Dorado

1 ½ oz. Sauza Conmemorativo tequila
½ oz. Chambord
½ oz. peach puree
½ oz. sweet and sour mix

Friar Tuck

1 oz. Kahlúa
¾ oz. Frangelico
½ oz. cream
Maraschino cherry for garnish

Frosted Romance

1 oz. Chambord
1 oz. vanilla ice cream
1 oz. white crème de cacao
Maraschino cherry for garnish

Frosty Comfort

1 cup orange juice
1 cup orange sherbet
1 oz. Southern Comfort

Frosty Friar

1 ½ oz. Frangelico liqueur
1 oz. strawberry ice cream
¾ oz. white rum

Frozen Apple

1 ½ oz. Laird's applejack
1 ½ oz. sweet and sour mix
1 oz. lime juice
½ tsp. superfine sugar

Frozen Apricot Sour

2 oz. orange juice
1 ½ oz. apricot brandy
1 ½ oz. prepared limeade
1 tsp. superfine sugar

Frozen Aquavit

1 oz. Aquavit
1 oz. sweet and sour mix

Frozen Berkeley

2 oz. light rum
½ oz. brandy
1 tbsp. lime juice
1 tbsp. passion fruit syrup

Frozen California Sour

2 oz. orange juice
1 ½ oz. bourbon
1 tsp. superfine sugar

Frozen Fuzzy

1 oz. lemon-lime soda
¾ oz. peach schnapps
¼ oz. Cointreau
Splash grenadine
Splash lime juice

Frozen Golden

3 oz. vanilla ice cream
1 ½ oz. Galliano
½ oz. white crème de cacao
Maraschino cherry for garnish

Frozen Hurricane

1 oz. gold rum
1 oz. light rum
1 oz. lime juice
1 oz. orange juice
½ oz. passion fruit syrup
¼ oz. grenadine

Frozen Mexican Coffee

4 oz. strong coffee
2 oz. Frangelico liqueur
1 ½ oz. Coco Lopez cream of coconut
1 oz. chocolate syrup

Frozen Mint Julep

2 oz. bourbon
1 oz. lemon juice
1 oz. sugar syrup
5-6 mint leaves

Frozen Peachy Orange Colada

2 oz. Coco Lopez cream of coconut
2 oz. orange juice
1 ½ oz. peach schnapps
½ oz. grenadine

Frozen Pine

2 oz. pineapple juice
1 oz. Canadian Mist
1 oz. grenadine
Maraschino cherry for garnish

Frozen Pink Squirrel

3 oz. vanilla ice cream
1 oz. crème de noyaux
½ oz. white crème de cacao

Frozen Rhumba

2 oz. orange juice
2 oz. triple sec
1 ½ oz. Bacardi light rum
1 oz. grapefruit juice
½ oz. lime juice

Frozen Scotch

1 oz. lemon juice
1 ¼ oz. scotch
1 tsp. superfine sugar

Frozen Scotch Sour

2 oz. orange juice
1 ½ oz. scotch

Fruit Salad

1 ½ oz. DeKuyper Pucker Cheri-Beri
½ oz. DeKuyper Pucker grape
½ oz. Peachtree schnapps
Splash orange juice

Funky Monkey

½ fresh ripe banana, peeled
¾ oz. crème de banana
¾ oz. rum
¾ oz. white crème de cacao
Banana slices for garnish

Funky Monkey II

2 oz. Kahlúa
1 oz. brandy
1 oz. crème de banana
½ oz. ice cream
Maraschino cherry for garnish

Fuzzless Screwdriver

2 oz. orange juice
1 ½ oz. Hiram Walker Jubilee peach
    schnapps
1 oz. vodka

Fuzzy Fruit

4 oz. orange juice
2 oz. half-and-half
2 oz. peach nectar
¾ oz. amaretto liqueur
¾ oz. peach schnapps
Maraschino cherry for garnish

Galliano Colada

2 oz. pineapple juice
1 oz. coconut milk
¾ oz. Galliano
¾ oz. Mount Gay rum
Pineapple wedge and maraschino cherry
    for garnish

Serve with straws.

Galliano Milkshake

2–2 ½ oz. vanilla ice cream, depending
    upon desired thickness
2 oz. Galliano

 MRS. JOHN LOCKLEY • SAN FRANCISCO, CA

Galliano Sunshine

1 ¼ oz. Galliano
1 oz. orange sherbet

Gaugin

2 oz. light rum
1 oz. passion fruit syrup
1 tsp. grenadine
1 tsp. lime juice or juice of ½ lime
½ tsp. superfine sugar

Gay Galliano

1 ½ oz. Mount Gay rum
¾ oz. Galliano
½ oz. lime juice
Slice of lime and maraschino cherry for
    garnish

Georgia Peach

1 ½ oz. Bacardi light or dark rum
¾ oz. orange juice
½ oz. peach brandy
Peach slice for garnish

German Chocolate Cake

⅓ oz. Frangelico
⅓ oz. Kahlúa
⅓ oz. light crème de cacao
¼ oz. cream
½ oz. ice

German Peach

1 ½ oz. vodka
1 oz. peach brandy
1 tsp. lemon juice
1 tsp. peach preserves
Fresh peach slice for garnish

Giada

¾ oz. vodka
½ oz. Campari
½ oz. Galliano
¼ oz. pineapple juice
Maraschino cherry for garnish

Gin Fizz

2 oz. dry gin
Juice of ½ lemon
Juice of ½ lime
1 tbsp. confectioners' sugar
Club soda to fill

Ginger Colada

1 ½ oz. Canton Delicate ginger liqueur
1 oz. pineapple juice
1 oz. rum
1 ½ tbsp. Coco Lopez cream of coconut

Go Go Cherry Juice

3 oz. pineapple guava nectar
1 oz. maraschino cherry juice
1 oz. vodka
1 tbsp. Coco Lopez cream of coconut
Three maraschino cherries for garnish

 MARILY CECCONE • WESTBURY, NY

Godiva Irish Freeze

1 ½ oz. Godiva liqueur
¾ oz. Irish cream liqueur
Maraschino cherry for garnish

Godiva Whisper

3 oz. vanilla ice cream
¾ oz. Godiva liqueur
½ oz. Martell cognac
Maraschino cherry for garnish

Golden Cadillac

2 oz. Galliano
1 oz. half-and-half
1 oz. white crème de cacao

Golden Chain

1 part Galliano
1 part Rémy Martin cognac
¾ part fresh lime juice
Slice of lime and maraschino cherry for
    garnish

Golden Fizzer

2 oz. rum
½ lemon, peeled
1 egg yolk
1 tsp. superfine sugar

Golden Gate

½ pint orange ice or sherbet
2 oz. gin or light rum

Golden Slipper

2 oz. apricot brandy
1 oz. yellow Chartreuse
1 egg yolk

Good and Plenty

1 oz. coffee liqueur
1 oz. vodka
½ oz. vanilla ice cream
Dash Pernod

Good Fortune

2 oz. vanilla ice cream
1 ½ oz. Devonshire cream liqueur
1 oz. Canton Delicate ginger liqueur
½ oz. rum
Three maraschino cherries for garnish

Goombay Smash

1 oz. Coco Lopez cream of coconut
1 oz. dark rum
1 oz. light rum
1 oz. pineapple juice

Gorky Park Cooler

4 oz. pineapple juice
1 ½ oz. Stoli Strasberi vodka
½ oz. coconut rum
½ oz. spiced rum

Grab My Coconuts

2 ½ oz. Bartenders Good Time coconut rum
1 oz. Bacardi light
1 oz. pineapple juice

 TIM LOWERY • WI

Grand Finale

2 oz. Coco Lopez cream of coconut
1 oz. almond liqueur
1 oz. hazelnut liqueur
1 oz. light cream
Grated nutmeg for garnish

Grand Marnier Margarita

1 oz. freshly squeezed lime juice
1 oz. Grand Marnier
1 oz. super premium tequila
Superfine sugar to taste

Grapefruit Fizz

1 cup grapefruit juice
2 oz. sherry wine
1 egg white
1 tbsp. superfine sugar

Grasshopper

2 oz. heavy cream
1 oz. green crème de menthe
1 oz. white crème de cacao

Green Elevator (Chartreuse Cocktail)

2 oz. green Chartreuse
Juice of 1 lemon
1 egg white
2 tbsp. grapefruit juice

Green Eyes

1 ½ oz. pineapple juice
1 oz. rum
¾ oz. Midori melon liqueur
½ oz. Coco Lopez cream of coconut
½ oz. Rose's lime juice

Groundhog's Shadow

2 oz. DeKuyper root beer schnapps
2 oz. light cream
1 oz. Gilbey's gin

Guava Colada

2 oz. guava nectar
1 ½ oz. Coco Lopez cream of coconut
1 ¼ oz. vodka or rum

Guillotine

2 oz. Mandarine Napoleon
1 oz. pineapple juice
½ oz. gin
½ oz. white rum

Harbor Lights

1 oz. DeKuyper light crème de cacao
1 oz. Puerto Rican rum
1 oz. tequila

Harvest Moon

2 oz. brandy
1 oz. Mandarine Napoleon
Dash lemon juice
Lemon twist for garnish

Havana Banana Fizz

2 ½ oz. pineapple juice
2 oz. light rum
1 ½ oz. fresh lime juice
⅓ banana, sliced
3–5 dashes Peychaud's bitters
Bitter lemon soda to fill

Havana Special

4 oz. white rum
1 oz. lemon juice or lime juice
1 tbsp. maraschino liqueur
½ tbsp. superfine sugar

Hawaiian Daisy

1 ½ oz. Bacardi light rum
1 oz. pineapple juice
¼ oz. grenadine
¼ oz. lemon juice or lime juice
1 egg white
Club soda to fill

Hawaiian Eye

1 ½ oz. bourbon
1 oz. heavy cream
1 oz. Kahlúa
½ oz. crème de banana
½ oz. vodka
1 tsp. Pernod
Maraschino cherry and pineapple spear for
    garnish

Hawaiian Holiday

1 ½ oz. Bacardi light or dark rum
1 ½ oz. guava juice
1 oz. grapefruit juice
Dash bitters

Hawaiian Punch

3 oz. Coco Lopez cream of coconut
3 oz. gin or rum
1 jigger lemon juice
2 tsp. superfine sugar
1 tsp. Grand Marnier
Maraschino cherry and pineapple spear for
   garnish

Hawaiian Sunset

3 oz. orange juice
1 ½ oz. sweet and sour mix
1 oz. gin
Dash grenadine
Orange wedge and maraschino cherry for
   garnish

Heather's Dream

½ oz. canned peach or ½ ripe peach peeled
½ oz. heavy cream
½ oz. Romana sambuca
Maraschino cherry for garnish

Heavenly Ginger

1 oz. Canton Delicate ginger liqueur
1 oz. Devonshire cream liqueur

Hibiscus

2 oz. orange juice
½ oz. brandy or cognac
½ oz. Grand Marnier
½ oz. lemon juice
½ oz. lime juice

Ho Ho and a Barrel of Rum

1 ½ oz. Hiram Walker Old Fashioned root
   beer schnapps
1 oz. milk or cream
1 oz. rum

Holiday Winter Mint

⅔ oz. cream
⅔ oz. Du Bouchett green crème de menthe
⅔ oz. Vandermint liqueur
Maraschino cherry for garnish

Honey Bee

1 ½ oz. Bacardi light rum
¾ oz. cream
¾ oz. honey
¾ oz. lemon juice or lime juice

Honeydew Daiquiri

1 oz. Midori melon liqueur
1 oz. sweet and sour lemon
½ oz. white rum

Honeysuckle Rose

1 ½ oz. Bacardi dark rum
¾ oz. lemon juice or lime juice
½ oz. grenadine
½ oz. honey

Honolulu Cocktail

1 ½ oz. Bacardi light or dark rum
1 oz. lemon juice or lime juice
1 oz. orgeat syrup
1 oz. pineapple juice
½ oz. grenadine
Dash bitters

Hop Scotch

1 ½ oz. pineapple juice
1 oz. Coco Lopez cream of coconut
¾ oz. blackberry brandy
¾ oz. scotch
¼ oz. lemon juice

Hot Dutch Hug

2 oz. Vandermint liqueur
1 oz. Du Bouchett crème de almond liqueur
1 oz. hot chocolate

Hot Lips

2 oz. orange juice
2 oz. Passoã
½ oz. tequila
1 oz. cranberry juice
Orange slice for garnish
Strawberry for garnish

Serve in a short tumbler glass.

Hot Rum Cow

2 oz. light rum
1 oz. milk
2 tsp. superfine sugar
¼ tsp. vanilla extract

Hummer

2 oz. vanilla or chocolate ice cream
1 oz. Kahlúa
½ oz. rum
Maraschino cherry for garnish

Hurrah Milk Punch

4 oz. milk
2 oz. whiskey
1 tsp. sugar syrup
½ tsp. Jamaican rum

Iceball

1 shot gin
½ shot sambuca
½ shot white crème de menthe
Splash cream

Icebreaker

2 oz. grapefruit juice
2 oz. tequila
¾ oz. grenadine
½ oz. Cointreau

Ich Bien

2 oz. apple brandy
2 oz. half-and-half
1 egg yolk
½ oz. white Curaçao
Grated nutmeg for garnish

Icy Brendan's

3 oz. Saint Brendan's Superior Irish cream
2 oz. vanilla ice cream
Maraschino cherry for garnish

Il Magnifico

1 oz. Cointreau
1 oz. cream
1 oz. Tuaca
Maraschino cherry for garnish

Illusion

2 oz. pineapple juice
1 oz. Coco Lopez cream of coconut
½ oz. Cointreau
½ oz. Midori melon liqueur
½ oz. vodka

In the Pink

1 ¼ oz. Myers's Original rum cream
1 oz. Coco Lopez cream of coconut
1 tsp. grenadine

International Cream

2 oz. vanilla ice cream
½ oz. Carolans Irish cream
½ oz. Kahlúa
Splash Grand Marnier
Splash milk

International Mai Tai

2 oz. pineapple juice
2 oz. sweet and sour mix
½ oz. Malibu rum
½ oz. Myers's dark rum
½ oz. rum
1 tsp. orgeat syrup

Irish Angel

1 oz. Bushmills Irish whiskey
¼ oz. white crème de cacao
¼ oz. white crème de menthe
½ oz. cream
Maraschino cherry for garnish

Irish Berry

1 ½ oz. strawberries
1 oz. Coco Lopez cream of coconut
1 oz. Irish cream liqueur
½ oz. vodka
Dash grenadine

Irish Dream

1 oz. vanilla ice cream
½ oz. Carolans Irish cream
½ oz. Hiram Walker dark crème de cacao
½ oz. Hiram Walker hazelnut liqueur
Maraschino cherry for garnish

Irish Eyes

2 oz. heavy cream
1 oz. Irish whiskey
¼ oz. green crème de menthe
Maraschino cherry for garnish

Irish Fix

2 oz. Irish whiskey
1 oz. Irish Mist
½ oz. fresh lemon juice
½ oz. pineapple juice
Lemon slice, orange slice, and pineapple
    spear for garnish

Irish Kilt

1 ½ oz. sugar syrup or to taste
1 oz. Irish whiskey
1 oz. lemon juice
1 oz. scotch
3-4 dashes orange bitters

Irish Lace

3 oz. pineapple juice
2 oz. Coco Lopez cream of coconut
2 oz. half-and-half
1 oz. Irish Mist
Orange flag for garnish

Irish Rainbow

1 ½ oz. Irish whiskey
3-4 dashes Angostura bitters
3-4 dashes maraschino liqueur
3-4 dashes orange Curaçao
3-4 dashes Pernod
Strip of orange peel

Twist orange peel over drink and drop in.

Irish Raspberry

1 oz. Devonshire Irish cream
½ oz. Chambord

Irish Shillelagh

¼ cup peaches, fresh or canned, diced
1 ½ oz. Irish whiskey
1 oz. lemon juice or juice of ½ lemon
½ oz. light rum
½ oz. sloe gin
1 tsp. powdered sugar
Fresh raspberries for garnish

Island Pleasure

2 oz. heavy cream
1 ½ oz. Angostura grenadine
1 oz. crème de banana
¼ oz. Frangelico

Isle of Pines

2 oz. light rum
½ oz. fresh lime juice
1 tsp. peppermint schnapps
6 fresh mint leaves

Isle of the Blessed Coconut

2 oz. light rum
1 oz. Coco Lopez cream of coconut
½ oz. fresh lemon juice
½ oz. fresh lime juice
½ oz. fresh orange juice
1 tsp. orgeat syrup

Italian Alexander

2 oz. half-and-half
1 oz. vanilla ice cream
¾ oz. Disaronno amaretto
¾ oz. white crème de cacao
Grated nutmeg for garnish

Italian Banana

2 oz. orange juice
1 oz. sweet and sour mix
¾ shot amaretto
¾ shot crème de banana
Maraschino cherry for garnish

Italian Bushwacker

2 oz. half-and-half
½ oz. Carolans Irish cream
½ oz. Hiram Walker amaretto liqueur
½ oz. Kahlúa
½ oz. white rum
Maraschino cherry for garnish

Italian Colada

2 oz. pineapple juice
1 ½ oz. Puerto Rican white rum
¾ oz. heavy cream
¼ oz. amaretto
¼ oz. Coco Lopez cream of coconut

Italian Margarita

2 oz. sweet and sour mix
1 oz. Disaronno amaretto
½ oz. tequila
½ oz. triple sec

Italian Orange Blossom

1 ½ oz. Galliano
1 oz. orange juice
Dash tequila

 MRS. SOPHIA DODGE • DALY CITY, CA

Jack Rose

2 oz. applejack brandy
1 oz. lime or lemon juice
2 tbsp. grenadine syrup
1 egg white

Jamaica Snow

2 oz. Appleton white rum
2 oz. Coco Lopez cream of coconut
1 ¼ oz. Rose's lime juice
Lime wheel and crushed pineapple for
   garnish

Jamaican Blues

2 cups ice
2 oz. Coco Lopez cream of coconut
2 oz. pineapple juice
1 ¼ oz. rum
½ oz. blue Curaçao

Jamaican Breeze

5 oz. pineapple juice
1 ¼ oz. Frangelico
¾ oz. Bols ginger brandy
½ oz. Coco Lopez cream of coconut
½ oz. lime juice

Jamaican Shake

2 oz. milk or cream
1 shot Myers's dark rum
½ shot blended whiskey

Jelly Donut

3 oz. raspberry sorbet
1 ¼ oz. Disaronno amaretto
¾ oz. Chambord
½ oz. vanilla ice cream

Jocko's Julep

3 oz. bourbon
1 oz. green crème de menthe
1 ½ oz. fresh lime juice
1 tsp. superfine sugar
5 fresh mint leaves
Sparkling water to fill
Mint sprig for garnish

John Collins

2 oz. bourbon whiskey
½ lemon, peeled
1 tsp. superfine sugar

Jungle Jim

2 oz. crème de banana
2 oz. milk
2 oz. vodka

Jungle Juice

1 ½ oz. cranberry juice
1 ½ oz. freshly squeezed orange juice
1 ½ oz. Jose Cuervo gold tequila
1 ½ oz. pineapple juice
Lemon or lime soda to fill

Kahlúa and Cream

3 oz. cream
1 ½ oz. Kahlúa
½ oz. crushed ice

Kahlúa Banana

1 fresh banana
2 oz. Coco Lopez cream of coconut
2 oz. pineapple juice
1 ½ oz. Kahlúa
¾ oz. rum

Kahlúa Banana Cream Fizz

1 banana, sliced
2 oz. half-and-half
2 oz. Kahlúa
1 oz. rum
¾ oz. lime juice
Club soda to fill

Kahlúa Blizzard

4 oz. Coco Lopez cream of coconut
1 ½ oz. Kahlúa
1 oz. white crème de menthe
Whipped cream and shredded coconut for
    garnish

Kahlúa Brandy Alexander

4 oz. vanilla ice cream
1 oz. brandy or cognac
1 oz. Kahlúa

Kahlúa Cane

1 ¼ oz. Kahlúa
½ oz. peppermint schnapps
Crushed candy cane

Kahlúa Cherry Fizz

1 ½ oz. Kahlúa
1 ½ oz. milk or cream
Splash of cherry cola
Maraschino cherry for garnish

Kahlúa Chi Chi

2 oz. pineapple juice
1 oz. Coco Lopez cream of coconut
1 oz. Kahlúa
¾ oz. vodka

Kahlúa Chocolate Almond

1 ½ oz. Kahlúa
¾ oz. amaretto
½ oz. cream
Splash of cherry cola
Maraschino cherry for garnish

Blend the first three ingredients. Splash cola and top with a maraschino cherry.

Kahlúa Coconut Mudslide

1 oz. Coco Lopez cream of coconut
1 oz. milk or cream
1 oz. vodka
½ oz. Carolans Irish cream
½ oz. Kahlúa

Kahlúa Cognac & Cream

2 oz. cream or milk
1 oz. Kahlúa
½ oz. cognac
Dollop of whipped cream and maraschino
    cherry for garnish

Kahlúa Colada

2 oz. Coco Lopez cream of coconut
2 oz. pineapple juice
1 ½ oz. Kahlúa
1 oz. light rum
Maraschino cherry and pineapple wedge
    for garnish

Kahlúa Cream Soda

2 oz. cream
1 ½ oz. Kahlúa
Cub soda to fill
Maraschino cherry for garnish

Kahlúa Creamsicle

1 ½ oz. Kahlúa
1 oz. orange juice
½ oz. milk or cream
Slice of orange for garnish

Kahlúa Dublin Banana

1 banana
1 oz. Irish cream
1 oz. Kahlúa
½ oz. half-and-half
Banana sliver for garnish

Kahlúa Fuzz Buster

1 ½ oz. Kahlúa
1 oz. heavy cream
1 oz. soda
½ oz. peach schnapps
Club soda to fill
Slice of peach for garnish

Kahlúa Kialoa

1 ½ oz. dark rum
1 ½ oz. Kahlúa
1 oz. heavy cream

Kahlúa Mudslide

1 oz. milk or cream
1 oz. vodka
½ oz. Irish cream liqueur
½ oz. Kahlúa

Kahlúa Peanut Butter Cocktail

1 ½ oz. heavy cream
1 ½ oz. Kahlúa
½ oz. tequila
1 tbsp. creamy peanut butter

Kahlúa Peppermint Patty

2 oz. vanilla ice cream
1 oz. Kahlúa
½ oz. white crème de menthe
Mint leaf for garnish

Kahlúa Polar Bear

2 oz. vanilla ice cream
1 oz. Kahlúa
1 oz. vodka

Kahlúa Stinger

1 ¾ oz. Kahlúa
¾ oz. white crème de menthe

Kahlúa Strawberries & Cream

1 ½ oz. Kahlúa
1 oz. strawberry schnapps
Half-and-half to fill
Strawberry for garnish

Kahlúa Strawberry Colada

2 oz. pineapple juice
1 ½ oz. Kahlúa
1 oz. Coco Lopez cream of coconut
1 oz. light rum
Fresh strawberries or 4 oz. strawberry
   schnapps
Strawberry or pineapple wedge for garnish

Kahlúa Strawberry Cream Daiquiri

1 ½ oz. Kahlúa
1 oz. half-and-half
½ oz. rum
½ oz. lime juice
4 medium, ripe strawberries, plus 1 for garnish

Kahlúa Toasted Almond

2 oz. cream or milk
1 oz. Kahlúa
½ oz. Disaronno amaretto

Kahlúa Top Banana

2 oz. milk or cream
1 ½ oz. Kahlúa
1 oz. crème de banana

Kahlúa Toreador

2 oz. brandy
1 oz. Kahlúa
½ egg white

Kahlúa White

2 oz. milk or cream
1 oz. Kahlúa
½ oz. light rum

Kalada

2 oz. pineapple juice
1 oz. Coco Lopez cream of coconut
1 oz. Kahlúa
½ oz. Myers's rum

Karamazov Koffee

1 oz. Disaronno amaretto
1 oz. Stoli Kafya vodka
1 oz. white crème de cacao

Key Largo

2 oz. dark rum
1 oz. Coco Lopez cream of coconut
1 oz. orange sherbet
Slice of orange for garnish

Key Lime Dream

2 oz. vanilla ice cream
1 ½ oz. light rum
¾ oz. Rose's lime juice

Key West Freeze

2 oz. orange juice
1 ½ oz. Coco Lopez cream of coconut
1 ¼ oz. Frangelico
¼ oz. blue Curaçao
¼ oz. Rose's lime juice

Killer Colada

2 cups crushed ice
3 oz. Whaler's Killer coconut rum
3 tbsp. coconut milk
3 tbsp. pineapple, crushed
Pineapple wedge for garnish

King Alexander

1 oz. gin
1 oz. vanilla ice cream
1 oz. white crème de cacao
Freshly grated nutmeg for garnish

Kingston

1 oz. Appleton Jamaican rum
½ oz. Tanqueray gin
Juice of ½ lime or lemon
1 tsp. grenadine

Kingston Combo

4 oz. pineapple juice
2 oz. Appleton dark Jamaican rum
½ oz. lime juice
Maraschino cherry or pineapple spear for
    garnish

Kiss o' the Nile

½ pint lemon-lime sherbet
2 oz. gin
Mint leaf for garnish

Kocktail Kid

1 oz. Captain Morgan spiced rum
1 oz. maraschino cherry juice
1 oz. pineapple juice
1 oz. sweet and sour mix
½ oz. triple sec

Serve in a martini glass.

 MOHSEN ALAM EL DIN • MT. KISCO, NY

Kremlin Cocktail

2 oz. vodka
1 ½ oz. half-and-half
1 ½ oz. white crème de cacao

La Bamba

3 oz. orange juice
1 ½ oz. banana
1 oz. Sauza extra gold
½ oz. Frangelico
Splash of 7-Up

Blend the first four ingredients. Add a splash of 7-Up.

La Bamba Margarita

1 ½ oz. orange juice
1 ¼ oz. Sauza Conmemorativo tequila
½ oz. Hiram Walker triple sec
¼ oz. grenadine
¼ oz. pineapple juice
Pineapple wedge for garnish

La Dolce Vita

3 oz. coffee ice cream
1 ½ oz. Hiram Walker Sambuca
Maraschino cherry for garnish

La Florida

4 oz. white rum
2 oz. Curaçao
1 oz. lemon or lime juice
1 tbsp. orange juice
2 tsp. superfine sugar

La Vie En Rose

1 oz. gin
1 oz. Kirsch
1 oz. lemon juice
½ oz. grenadine

Labadu

3 oz. Malibu rum
3 oz. pineapple juice
1 oz. milk or vanilla ice cream, depending
    upon desired thickness

Lady Luck

2 oz. cream
½ oz. Hiram Walker amaretto
½ oz. Hiram Walker blackberry brandy
½ oz. Hiram Walker Sambuca
Maraschino cherry for garnish

Latin Love

1 ½ oz. Jose Cuervo Especial tequila
1 oz. Disaronno amaretto
½ 6-oz. can Coco Lopez cream of coconut
Slice of orange or lemon for garnish
Coarse sugar for rim

Serve in a bell glass with the rim dipped in amaretto and then in sugar.

Lava Flow

½ banana
2 oz. colada mix (pineapple juice and
   coconut syrup)
1 ¼ oz. light rum
1 oz. liquid ice cream
¼ cup strawberry puree

Blend banana, colada mix, rum, and ice cream. Pour strawberry puree into a glass about ⅛ full, then pour blended mixture over the top to create a swirl.

Lava Glow

1 oz. sloe gin
1 oz. orange juice
2 oz. ginger ale
4 maraschino cherries, plus one for garnish
Whipped cream for garnish

Blend gin and orange juice. Add ginger ale.
Serve topped with whipped cream and a cherry.

 ROSE MUZIKA • UNIONTOWN, PA

Lazzaroni French Connection

2 parts Ansac cognac
1 part Lazzaroni amaretto

Lazzaroni Frost

½ cup plain yogurt
2 oz. orange juice
1 ½ oz. Lazzaroni amaretto
1 oz. coconut cream

Leprechaun

¼ fresh peach, peeled and diced
2 oz. Irish whiskey
1 oz. fresh lemon juice
1 oz. light rum
½ oz. sloe gin
½ tsp. superfine sugar
Fresh raspberries for garnish

Leprechaun's Libation

2 ½ oz. Bushmills Irish whiskey
½ oz. green crème de menthe

Licorice Mist

2 oz. Coco Lopez cream of coconut
2 oz. half-and-half
1 ½ oz. Romana sambuca

Licorice with a Twist

3 oz. coffee ice cream
1 ½ oz. Hiram Walker licorice schnapps

Lifesaver

2 oz. orange juice
2 oz. pineapple juice
1 oz. Smirnoff vodka
1 oz. triple sec
½ tsp. grenadine

Lighthouse Laddie

2 oz. Coco Lopez cream of coconut
2 oz. half-and-half
1 oz. dark crème de cacao
1 oz. rum
½ oz. butterscotch schnapps

Lime Daiquiri

4 oz. sweet and sour mix
1 ¼ oz. rum
Juice ½ fresh lime
Lime wheel for garnish

Limey

2 oz. light rum
½ oz. triple sec
1 tbsp. lime juice
Slice of lime for garnish

Lipshitz Libation

3 oz. half-and-half
1 ½ oz. Puerto Rican rum
1 oz. Disaronno amaretto

London Fog

1 oz. Pernod
1 oz. vanilla ice cream
1 oz. white crème de menthe

Long Stemmed Rose

4 oz. whole milk
2 oz. strawberry ice cream
1 ½ oz. Tequila Rose
1 oz. Nesquik strawberry syrup
½ oz. ice
4 maraschino cherries, stems removed, for
  garnish
Whipped cream for garnish

Pour into a hurricane glass. Top with whipped
cream and two maraschino cherries.

 JEANNE MARIE GENDREAU • OWASSO, OK

Louisiana Lady

1 ½ oz. Bacardi light rum
1 egg white
¾ oz. lemon juice or lime juice
½ tsp. superfine sugar
Dash Peychaud's bitters

Love Potion

1 oz. orange juice
1 oz. pineapple juice
1 oz. rum
½ oz. crème de banana
½ oz. triple sec
Orange slice, pineapple wedge, and slice of
    banana for garnish

Lt. Kije's Kolada

3 oz. pineapple juice
¼ cup fresh strawberries
1 ½ oz. Stoli Strasberi vodka
1 oz. Coco Lopez cream of coconut
½ oz. light rum
½ oz. small ripe banana

Lucky Irish

1 ½ oz. Irish whiskey
1 oz. Angostura lime juice
½ oz. Angostura grenadine
½ oz. light rum
⅓ oz. sloe gin
2 peach slices (diced), 5 to 6 fresh raspber-
    ries, and 1 maraschino cherry for garnish

Lucky Lady

¾ oz. Bacardi light-dry rum
¾ oz. cream
¼ oz. Hiram Walker white crème de cacao
¼ oz. Romana sambuca
Maraschino cherry for garnish

Magpie

1 oz. Midori melon liqueur
1 oz. vodka
¾ oz. cream
½ oz. white crème de cacao
Maraschino cherry for garnish

Mahogany Mauler

1 oz. cherry brandy
1 oz. orange juice
1 oz. vodka

Mahukona

2 oz. light rum
½ tsp. almond syrup
½ oz. freshly squeezed lemon juice
½ oz. white Curaçao
5 dashes orange bitters
Pineapple spear for garnish

Mai Tai

3 oz. pineapple juice
1 ¼ oz. Malibu rum
1 oz. sweet and sour mix
¾ oz. dark rum
Pineapple slice, orange slice, and cherry
   for garnish

Major Margarita

4 oz. Major Peters' margarita mix
1 ½ oz. Jose Cuervo tequila
½ oz. Major Peters' lime juice

Major Strawberry Margarita

½ cup strawberries (fresh or frozen)
   or 4 oz. Major Peters' strawberry
   margarita mix
1 ½ oz. Jose Cuervo tequila
½ oz. Major Peters' lime juice

Malibu California Coastline

2 oz. pineapple juice
2 oz. sweet and sour mix
1 oz. Malibu rum
1 oz. peach schnapps
½ oz. blue Curaçao
Pineapple wedge for garnish

Malibu Caribbean Cooker

2 oz. Malibu rum
½ ripe banana
½ oz. vanilla ice cream

Malibu Coconut Colada

4 oz. Coco Lopez cream of coconut
2 oz. Malibu rum
2 oz. orange juice
1 oz. half-and-half
Toasted coconut for garnish

Malibu Conga Punch

3 oz. Malibu rum
2 oz. grapefruit juice
2 oz. orange juice
2 oz. pineapple juice
Dash bitters

Malibu Mai Tai

2 oz. pineapple juice
2 oz. sweet and sour mix
½ oz. Malibu rum
½ oz. Myers's dark rum
½ oz. rum

Malibu Margarita

2 oz. lime juice
1 ½ oz. Malibu rum
1 oz. Cointreau

Malibu Orange Colada

3 oz. Coco Lopez cream of coconut
1 ½ oz. Malibu rum
1 oz. triple sec

Malibu Shake

3 oz. pineapple juice
2 oz. cream
1 ½ oz. Malibu rum
1 oz. white crème de menthe

Malibu Slide

Equal parts:
Baileys Irish cream
Kahlúa
Malibu rum

Malibu Smooth Grove

1 ½ oz. Baileys Irish cream
1 ½ oz. Malibu rum
1 ½ oz. Midori melon liqueur
½ oz. vanilla ice cream

Malibu Sunset

2 oz. orange juice
1 ½ oz. Malibu rum
1 oz. pineapple juice
2-3 oz. strawberries
Splash heavy cream
Maraschino cherry for garnish

Malibu Tropicale

2 oz. papaya juice
2 oz. pineapple juice
1 oz. Malibu rum
¾ oz. crème de banana
½ oz. Midori melon liqueur

Mandarinella

3 oz. Rémy Martin cognac
1 oz. Mandarine Napoleon
1 tsp. cream

Maraschino Cherry

1 oz. cranberry juice
1 oz. pineapple juice
¾ shot rum
¼ shot amaretto
¼ shot peach schnapps
Splash grenadine
Whipped cream and maraschino cherry for
    garnish

Margarita

1 oz. Cointreau
1 oz. sweet and sour mix or lime juice
1 oz. tequila
Lime wheel for garnish

Margarita Madness

3 oz. Coco Lopez margarita mix
1 ½ oz. tequila
½ oz. triple sec

Margarita Madres

1 ½ oz. cranberry juice
1 ½ oz. orange juice
1 ½ oz. sweet & sour mix
1 ¼ oz. Jose Cuervo gold tequila
½ oz. Cointreau
Slice of lime and maraschino cherry for garnish

Martha's Melons

2 oz. lemon mix
1 oz. Midori melon liqueur
1 oz. Puerto Rican rum
½ oz. sliced cantaloupe
½ oz. sliced honeydew melon
½ oz. sliced watermelon

Mary Rose

1 oz. cherry brandy
1 oz. gin
½ oz. port wine

Matador

2 oz. pineapple juice
1 oz. tequila
2 tsp. lime juice

Maui Breeze

2 oz. guava juice
2 oz. pineapple juice
½ oz. amaretto
½ oz. brandy
½ oz. Cointreau
1 oz. lemon juice or juice of ½ lemon
1 tsp. superfine sugar

Maui Fizz

1 oz. light rum
⅓ oz. dry sherry
Splash heavy cream
Orange slice and a maraschino cherry for
    garnish

Mello Mint

1 oz. Vandermint liqueur
½ oz. Du Bouchett melon liqueur
½ oz. Lazzaroni amaretto

Melon Colada

3 oz. Coco Lopez cream of coconut
2 oz. pineapple juice
1 oz. rum
¼ oz. Midori melon liqueur
Splash heavy cream
Maraschino cherry for garnish

Melon Colada II

4 oz. pineapple juice
2 oz. Coco Lopez cream of coconut
1 oz. light rum
1 oz. Midori melon liqueur
Maraschino cherry for garnish

Melon Cooler

4 oz. fresh melon (any kind)
2 oz. white wine
½ oz. Rose's grenadine
½ oz. Rose's lime juice

Melonhopper

1 oz. Midori melon liqueur
½ oz. heavy cream
½ oz. white crème de cacao

Metaxa Olympic Cocktail

3 oz. orange juice
¾ oz. Metaxa brandy
½ oz. Cointreau
Maraschino cherry for garnish

Mexican Mist

1 ½ oz. Sauza Conmemorativo tequila
½ oz. cranberry juice
½ oz. orange juice
½ oz. pineapple juice

Mexican Pain Killer

1 oz. pineapple juice
½ oz. gold tequila
½ oz. light rum
½ oz. orange juice
½ oz. vodka
2 tbsp. Coco Lopez cream of coconut
Maraschino cherry for garnish

Mexican Storm Cloud

2 oz. DeKuyper root beer schnapps
2 oz. Sauza tequila
1 oz. lime juice

Miami Fizz

1 ½ oz. Bacardi light or dark rum
1 oz. lemon juice
1 egg white
¼ oz. grenadine
¼ tsp. superfine sugar
Club soda to fill

Miami Ice

3 oz. pineapple juice
¾ oz. peach schnapps
¾ oz. rum
½ oz. Coco Lopez cream of coconut
¼ oz. grenadine
Club soda to fill

Miami Special

1 oz. Bacardi light-dry rum
¾ oz. lime juice
¼ oz. Hiram Walker white crème de menthe

Midnight Orchid

2 oz. pineapple juice
1 ½ oz. Finlandia cranberry vodka, chilled
½ oz. half-and-half
¼ oz. Chambord
Maraschino cherry for garnish

Midori Alexander

1 ½ oz. Midori melon liqueur
1 oz. brandy
1 oz. heavy cream
Maraschino cherry for garnish

Midori Cheap Shades

2 oz. orange juice
2 oz. pineapple juice
1 ¾ oz. Midori melon liqueur
1 oz. margarita mix
¾ oz. peach schnapps
Lemon-lime soda to fill

Midori Colada

2 oz. Coco Lopez cream of coconut
1 ½ oz. pineapple juice
1 oz. Midori melon liqueur
½ oz. Bacardi rum
Maraschino cherry and orange slice for
    garnish

Midori Daiquiri

1 oz. Midori melon liqueur
1 oz. sweet and sour mix
½ oz. white rum
Maraschino cherry for garnish

Midori Eggnog

2 oz. eggnog
1 oz. Midori melon liqueur
Grated nutmeg for garnish

Midori Frozen Melonball

4 oz. orange, pineapple, or grapefruit juice
2 oz. Midori melon liqueur
1 oz. vodka (optional)

Midori Frozen Sour

2 oz. sweet and sour mix
1 oz. Midori melon liqueur
Maraschino cherry and orange slice for
  garnish

Midori Green Iguana Margarita

2 oz. sweet and sour mix
1 oz. tequila
½ oz. Midori melon liqueur

Midori Hopper

1 oz. Midori melon liqueur
½ oz. white crème de menthe

Midori Magic

2 oz. heavy cream
2 oz. Midori melon liqueur
½ oz. Cointreau
Maraschino cherry for garnish

Midori Margarita

1 ½ oz. tequila
1 oz. Midori melon liqueur
1 oz. sweet and sour mix

Midori Sour

2 oz. sweet and sour mix
1 oz. Midori melon liqueur

Milky Way

1 oz. Cointreau
½ oz. dark crème de cacao
Whipped cream and maraschino cherry for
    garnish

Mint 'N Cream

3 oz. vanilla ice cream
1 ½ oz. Hiram Walker spearmint schnapps
Maraschino cherry for garnish

Mint Cocktail

2 oz. dry white wine
1 ½ oz. gin
½ oz. green crème de menthe
2 sprigs fresh mint for garnish

Mint Condition

3 oz. vanilla ice cream
¾ oz. bourbon
¾ oz. peppermint schnapps
¾ oz. vodka
½ oz. Kahlúa
Maraschino cherry for garnish

Mint Daiquiri

2 ½ oz. light rum
2 oz. lime juice
1 tsp. superfine sugar
6 mint leaves

Mint Julep (Blender Style)

2 tsp. confectioners' sugar
3 mint sprigs, plus 2 for garnish
Dash water
1 cup crushed ice
2 oz. Maker's Mark bourbon

Place three mint sprigs, water, and 1 teaspoon of the confectioners' sugar in a blender. Blend thoroughly. Add 1 cup crushed ice and bourbon. Blend a few seconds more. Pour into frosted glasses filled with crushed ice. Garnish with mint sprigs. Sprinkle remaining sugar on top. Serve with a straw.

Mississippi Mud

4 oz. vanilla ice cream
1 ½ oz. coffee liqueur
1 ½ oz. Southern Comfort
Maraschino cherry for garnish

Mist Cream

1 cup ice
4 oz. heavy cream
1 ½ oz. Canadian Mist
½ oz. coffee liqueur
Dash grenadine
Maraschino cherry for garnish

Mistral

2 oz. dry white wine
1 oz. Chambord
1 tbsp. frozen strawberries or raspberries

Monkey Special

2 oz. vanilla or chocolate ice cream
1 oz. dark rum
1 oz. light rum
½ oz. banana, peeled
Shaved chocolate for garnish

Mont Blanc

1 oz. Absolut vodka
1 oz. Chambord
1 oz. cream or half-and-half
1 oz. vanilla ice cream
Maraschino cherry for garnish

Montego Margarita

1 ½ oz. Appleton Estate rum
1 oz. crushed ice
1 oz. lemon or lime juice
½ oz. triple sec

Montezuma

2 oz. gold tequila
1 oz. Madeira wine
1 egg yolk

Montmartre

1 oz. Chambord
1 oz. heavy cream or half-and-half
1 oz. Hiram Walker coffee liqueur
Maraschino cherry for garnish

Montmartre Special

1 ½ oz. Bacardi light rum
¾ oz. cream
¼ oz. grenadine
Grated nutmeg for garnish

Moonlight

1 oz. Canton Delicate ginger liqueur
1 oz. dark crème de cacao
1 oz. heavy cream
Maraschino cherry for garnish

Morgan Cannonball

3 oz. pineapple juice
1 ¼ oz. Captain Morgan spiced rum
White crème de menthe for float

Blend the first two ingredients. Float crème de menthe on top.

Morgan Spiced Cream

2 oz. Captain Morgan spiced rum
2 oz. heavy cream, whipped stiffly
2 egg yolks
1 tsp. superfine sugar
Maraschino cherry for garnish

Morning Glory

2 oz. gin
1 egg
Juice of 1 lime
4 tsp. green crème de menthe

Morning Glory Daisy

2 oz. gin, brandy, or whiskey
2 tsp. Pernod
½ egg white
1 tsp. superfine sugar
Club soda to fill

Morning Midori

2 oz. orange juice
1 oz. Midori melon liqueur
½ oz. heavy cream
Maraschino cherry for garnish

Moscow Mimosa

3 oz. orange juice, chilled
1 ½ oz. vodka
Champagne to fill

Mozart Maraschino Struzzel Sip

1 oz. Frangelico
1 oz. heavy cream or milk
⅓ oz. Goldschläger
Dash cherry juice
Maraschino cherry for garnish

 NICOLA SWEET • FORT PIERCE, FL

Myers's Banana Daiquiri

½ sliced ripe banana
1 ½ oz. Myers's rum
½ oz. lemon juice
1 tsp. superfine sugar

Myers's Orange Daiquiri

1 ½ oz. Myers's rum
1 oz. orange juice
½ oz. lime juice
1 tsp. superfine sugar

Myers's Peach Daiquiri

2 oz. Myers's rum
2 fresh, peeled peach halves
1 oz. lime juice or lemon juice
1 tsp. superfine sugar

Myers's Piña Colada

2 oz. orange juice
2 oz. pineapple juice
1 ¼ oz. Myers's Original dark rum
1 oz. Coco Lopez cream of coconut
Maraschino cherry for garnish

Myers's Pineapple Daiquiri

2 oz. Myers's rum
½ slice of canned pineapple
1 tbsp. lime juice
1 tsp. superfine sugar
Maraschino cherry for garnish

Myers's Rum Cream Dream

1 ¼ oz. Myers's Original rum cream
1 oz. Coco Lopez cream of coconut
½ oz. chocolate syrup

Myers's Strawberry Daiquiri

½ cup strawberries
1 ¼ oz. Myers's dark rum
½ oz. Cointreau
Juice of ½ lime
1 tsp. superfine sugar

Neapolitan

1 ½ oz. Bacardi light or dark rum
½ oz. Grand Marnier
½ oz. lemon juice or lime juice
½ oz. triple sec

Nevada Cocktail

1 ½ oz. Bacardi light rum
¾ oz. grapefruit juice
½ oz. lemon juice or lime juice
½ tsp. superfine sugar
Dash bitters

New Orleans Night

2 oz. Coco Lopez cream of coconut
1 oz. half-and-half
1 oz. praline liqueur
1 oz. vodka
Maraschino cherry for garnish

New York White Colada

1 cup ice
4 oz. New York white table wine
½ oz. pineapple sherbet
¼ oz. fresh or canned pineapple with juice
Pineapple wedge and white grapes for garnish

New Yorker Highball

2 oz. bourbon
1 tsp. lemon juice
1 tsp. sugar syrup
Club soda to fill
1 oz. Claret for float

Blend the first three ingredients. Add club soda to fill the glass and float Claret on top.

Nuclear Reactor

1 ½ oz. Smirnoff vodka
½ oz. Bacardi light rum
½ oz. Coco Lopez cream of coconut
½ oz. Malibu rum

Nut and Honey

3 oz. vanilla ice cream
1 ½ oz. vodka
¾ oz. Frangelico
2 tbsp. honey
Maraschino cherry for garnish

Nutty Buddie

½ oz. Baileys Irish cream
½ oz. butterscotch schnapps
½ oz. Frangelico
½ oz. Kahlúa
½ oz. milk
Maraschino cherry for garnish

 GINA GEREMIA • JEANIE RYAN'S CAFE •
BRANFORD, CT

Nutty Colada

½ cup fresh or canned pineapple
2 oz. Coco Lopez cream of coconut
1 oz. Frangelico
1 oz. rum
Pineapple wedge, maraschino cherry, and
  shaved almonds for garnish

Nutty Colada II

2 oz. amaretto
2 oz. pineapple juice
1 oz. Coco Lopez Real Cream of Coconut
1 oz. gold rum
¼ tsp. crème de noyaux
Pineapple spear and maraschino cherry for
  garnish

Nutty Colada Easy

3 oz. pineapple juice
2 oz. amaretto
2 oz. Coco Lopez cream of coconut
Maraschino cherry for garnish

Nutty Squeeze

1 oz. amaretto
1 oz. fresh squeezed orange juice
1 oz. Marie Brizard Aphrodisiac
½ oz. sweet and sour mix

Obeah Princess

1 oz. Galliano
1 oz. Mount Gay rum
¾ oz. green crème de menthe
1 oz. egg white
Slice of orange for garnish

Old San Juan Sipper

1 ½ oz. Bacardi dark rum
1 oz. lemon or lime juice
½ oz. white crème de menthe
¼ oz. grenadine

Old Tavern Float

4 oz. orange juice
4 oz. orange sherbet
1 oz. DeKuyper root beer schnapps
1 oz. Gilbey's vodka

Olympics Cocktail

1 ½ oz. Bacardi dark rum
¾ oz. lemon juice or lime juice
½ oz. cherry brandy
Lemon or lime peel for garnish

Opal

1 oz. gin
1 oz. orange juice
1 tbsp. Cointreau
Few drops orange flower water

Orange Cadillac

1 ¼ oz. heavy cream
1 oz. Galliano
¾ oz. white crème de cacao
½ oz. orange juice

 JOE BEAUDRY • AUSTRALIA

Orange Daiquiri

2 oz. light rum
1 oz. orange juice
½ oz. lime juice
½ oz. triple sec

Orange Margarita

3 oz. orange juice
1 ½ oz. Jose Cuervo gold tequila
½ oz. Cointreau
½ oz. sweet and sour mix
Slice of orange for garnish

Orange Matador

1 ½ oz. tequila
1 oz. orange juice
1 oz. pineapple juice
1 tbsp. lime juice

Orange Smoothie

3 oz. Coco Lopez cream of coconut
3 oz. light cream
1 oz. Cointreau

Orange Velvet

½ oz. California white port
½ oz. orange juice
1 tbsp. lemon juice

Orange Vodka Delight

1 12-oz. can frozen orange juice
2 oz. Gordon's orange vodka
Slice of orange for garnish

Organ Grinder

2 oz. Coco Lopez cream of coconut
½ oz. dark rum
½ oz. light rum
¼ oz. rye whiskey
¼ oz. white crème de cacao

Oriental Cocktail

1 ½ oz. Bacardi light rum
¾ oz. orange juice
½ oz. cherry brandy
Maraschino cherry for garnish

Out of Bounds

Equal parts:
Kahlúa
Vodka
Butterscotch schnapps
Heavy cream or milk
Maraschino cherry for garnish

Paddler's Passion

1 oz. Bacardi amber rum
1 oz. vodka
1 ½ oz. orange juice
1 ½ oz. passion fruit juice
Dash coconut syrup
Dash grenadine
Pineapple wedge and maraschino cherry
  for garnish

Pamir Peach

2 oz. orange juice
1 oz. Disaronno amaretto
1 oz. Stoli Persik vodka
Dash lemon juice

Pancho's Pleasure

2 oz. Coco Lopez cream of coconut
1 oz. Irish cream liqueur
½ oz. almond liqueur
½ oz. coffee liqueur
½ oz. hazelnut liqueur

Panda Bear

2 oz. vanilla ice cream
1 oz. amaretto
1 oz. dark crème de cacao
Maraschino cherry for garnish

Pantomime

3 oz. dry vermouth
1 egg white
3–5 dashes grenadine
3–5 dashes orgeat syrup

Paradise Cocktail

1 oz. apricot brandy
1 oz. gin
1 oz. orange juice

Parisian Blonde

1 ½ oz. Bacardi light rum
¾ oz. cream
½ oz. orange Curaçao
Maraschino cherry for garnish

Passion Alessandro

1 oz. heavy cream
1 oz. Hiram Walker crème de cacao
1 oz. Opal Nera
Maraschino cherry for garnish

Passionate Margarita

1 ½ oz. Alizé
1 oz. lime juice
1 oz. tequila

Passoã Jungle Juice

3 oz. orange juice
2 oz. Passoã
1 oz. Galliano

Pavlova Peach

2 oz. cranberry juice
2 oz. orange juice
1 ½ oz. Stoli Persik vodka
Peach slice for garnish

Peach Alexander

3 oz. vanilla ice cream
1 oz. peach schnapps
½ fresh or canned peach
½ oz. white crème de cacao
Maraschino cherry for garnish

Peach Banana Daiquiri

¼ cup sliced peaches (fresh, frozen, or
   canned)
1 ½ oz. Puerto Rican light rum
1 oz. fresh lime juice
½ oz. medium banana, diced

Peach Daiquiri

½ peach, sliced
1 oz. lime juice
1 oz. rum
1 oz. triple sec
1 tsp. superfine sugar

Peach Irish

½ cup fresh lime juice
1 ripe peach (peeled, pitted, and sliced)
1 ½ oz. Irish whiskey
1 oz. apricot brandy
1 tbsp. superfine sugar
Dash vanilla extract

Peach Margarita

1 ½ oz. tequila
1 oz. lime juice or juice of ½ lime
1 oz. peach liqueur
1 tsp. triple sec
Salt and lime wedge to rim glass

Peach Melba

2 peach halves
2 oz. peach cocktail mix
1 oz. heavy cream
¾ oz. raspberry liqueur
½ oz. Captain Morgan spiced rum
Raspberry syrup for garnish

Peach Rumnog

1 fresh peach, pitted, or canned peach halves
2 oz. rum
1 egg
1 tbsp. superfine sugar
1 tsp. lemon juice

Peach Tree Cobbler

1 oz. apple barrel schnapps
1 oz. DeKuyper Peachtree schnapps

Peach Velvet

1 ½ oz. peach schnapps
½ oz. heavy cream
½ oz. white crème de cacao
Maraschino cherry for garnish

Peaches 'n Cream

3 oz. Coco Lopez cream of coconut
1 oz. peach schnapps
1 oz. rum
1 oz. vanilla ice cream
Maraschino cherry for garnish

Peachy Orange Colada

2 oz. Coco Lopez cream of coconut
2 oz. orange juice
1 ½ oz. peach schnapps
½ oz. grenadine
Maraschino cherry for garnish

Peanut Butter Cup

2 oz. Malibu rum
2 oz. vanilla ice cream
1 oz. Smirnoff vodka
2 tbsp. chocolate syrup
2 tbsp. creamy peanut butter

Peppermint Patty

1 oz. heavy cream
1 oz. peppermint schnapps
1 oz. white crème de cacao

Peppermint Stinger

1 ½ oz. brandy
1 oz. peppermint schnapps

Pernod Flip

2 oz. Pernod
1 egg
1 ½ oz. half-and-half
½ oz. orgeat syrup
Grated nutmeg for garnish

Piña Colada

2 oz. pineapple juice
1 ½ oz. rum
1 oz. Coco Lopez cream of coconut

Piña Koalapear

2 oz. DeKuyper Harvest Pear schnapps
1 oz. CocoRibe coconut rum
1 oz. cream
Maraschino cherry for garnish

Piñata

1 ½ oz. tequila
1 oz. lime juice
½ oz. crème de banana

Pineapple Bomb Margarita

3 oz. pineapple juice
1 oz. Grand Marnier
1 oz. Jose Cuervo tequila
½ oz. vodka

Pineapple Burster

½ oz. light rum
½ oz. Marie Brizard pineapple-coconut
½ oz. pineapple juice

Pineapple Cooler

2 oz. lime juice or lemon juice
1 oz. gin
1 oz. pineapple juice
½ oz. Jamaican rum
2 tsp. superfine sugar or grenadine

Pineapple Cooler II

2 slices fresh pineapple, cut in pieces
1 oz. gin
½ oz. green crème de menthe

Pineapple Daiquiri

3 oz. pineapple juice
1 ½ oz. light rum
1 oz. Rose's lime juice
½ oz. triple sec

Pineapple Mist

3 oz. pineapple juice
2 oz. light rum

Pink Cloud

2 oz. gin
2 oz. pineapple juice
1 egg white
1 oz. grenadine

Pink Elephant

½ fresh banana
2 oz. vanilla ice cream
1 oz. Appleton dark rum
1 oz. Wray & Nephew overproof rum
¾ oz. crème de banana
Splash crème de noya
Banana slice and maraschino cherry for
    garnish

Pink Lady

1 ½ oz. gin
1 ½ oz. vanilla ice cream
1 tsp. grenadine

Pink Lady Number One

1 egg white
1 oz. gin
1 tbsp. apple brandy
1 tbsp. grenadine syrup
1 tbsp. lemon juice

Pink Matador

2 oz. pineapple juice
1 ½ oz. Sauza tequila
½ oz. grenadine
½ oz. lime juice

Pink Panther

2 oz. heavy cream or half-and-half
1 ¼ oz. Sauza tequila
½ oz. grenadine

Pink Panther II

1 ¼ oz. Bacardi light rum
¾ oz. heavy cream
¾ oz. lemon juice
½ oz. Rose's grenadine

Pink Velvet

1 oz. heavy cream
1 oz. Hiram Walker chocolate cherry
½ oz. Hiram Walker crème de cassis

Pino Frio

2 oz. white rum
1 slice fresh pineapple
1 tbsp. superfine sugar

Pinsk Peach

1 ½ oz. Stoli Persik vodka
¾ oz. blue Curaçao
¼ oz. diced pineapple, fresh or canned
Dash lemon juice

Planter's Punch

2 oz. lime juice or lemon juice
1 ½ oz. Jamaican rum, plus ⅛ oz. for float
1 oz. orange juice
1 oz. pineapple juice
2 tsp. superfine sugar or grenadine

Blend all ingredients, reserving ⅛ ounce Jamaican rum. Float the remaining rum on top.

Platinum Blonde

1 ½ oz. Bacardi light or dark rum
¾ oz. heavy cream
½ oz. triple sec

Plum Goofer

1 cup ice
4 oz. Zinfandel
1-2 canned plums, seeded, plus 1 slice for
    garnish
2 oz. simple syrup
2 red seedless grapes for garnish

Poinciana

1 oz. apple juice
1 oz. light rum
2 maraschino cherries
½ oz. grenadine
Slice of orange for garnish

Polar Ice Cap

1 oz. Coco Lopez cream of coconut
1 oz. half-and-half
1 oz. vodka
½ oz. coffee liqueur

Polynesian Paradise

2 oz. Bacardi light or dark rum
2 oz. pineapple juice
1 oz. grenadine
1 oz. heavy cream
Pineapple spear and maraschino cherry for
    garnish

Polynesian Powerhouse

2 oz. Bacardi light or dark rum
1 oz. lemon or lime juice
1 oz. orange juice
1 oz. pineapple juice
½ oz. apricot brandy
½ oz. Bacardi 151 rum
½ oz. grenadine
2 dashes Angostura bitters
Fresh fruit slices (pineapple, lemons and
    limes, oranges, etc.) for garnish

Pompier Daisy

1 ½ oz. French vermouth
1 oz. crème de cassis
Cub soda to fill

Port and Sherry Cobbler

2 ½ oz. sherry
1 oz. port wine
½ tsp. Curaçao

Porto Flip

4 oz. port wine
1 oz. cognac
1 oz. thick cream
2 tsp. superfine sugar
Yellow Chartreuse for float

Blend everything but Yellow Chartreuse. Float
Yellow Chartreuse on top.

Presidente

1 oz. Bacardi rum
1 oz. dry vermouth
1 tsp. grenadine

Prince Igor's Nightcap

1 oz. Bombay Sapphire gin
1 oz. light cream
1 oz. Stoli Kafya vodka
Maraschino cherry for garnish

Princess Alexandra

1 ½ oz. Stoli Vanil vodka
1 oz. heavy cream or half-and-half
1 oz. white crème de cacao
Grated nutmeg for garnish

Puente Roman

2 oz. Harveys Bristol cream
1 ½ oz. heavy cream
1 ½ oz. orange juice
½ oz. brandy
Dash Hiram Walker orange Curaçao

Pump Room Alexander

3 oz. crème de cacao
3 oz. crème de menthe
3 oz. gin or brandy
3 oz. heavy cream
Maraschino cherry for garnish

Pushkin's Milk Shake

8 oz. cold milk or half-and-half
1 oz. Stoli Kafya vodka
1 oz. Stoli Ohranj vodka
Powdered cocoa for garnish

Racquet Ball Fizz

2 oz. grapefruit juice
1 ½ oz. Bacardi light rum
1 egg white
Club soda to fill

Raspberry Colada

2 oz. pineapple juice
1 ½ oz. Chambord
1 ½ oz. rum
1 oz. Coco Lopez cream of coconut

Raspberry Delight

1 oz. ice cream
¾ oz. Drambuie
¾ oz. Hiram Walker raspberry schnapps
½ oz. Tia Maria
Fresh raspberries for garnish

Raspberry Frost

2 oz. Coco Lopez cream of coconut
2 oz. light rum
1 oz. Chambord
Dash lime juice
Maraschino cherry for garnish

Raspberry Sweet Tart

1 oz. Angostura lime juice
1 oz. Chambord
1 oz. triple sec

Razberi Blow Pop

⅓ oz. Chambord
½ oz. crème de banana
½ oz. milk
½ oz. Peachtree schnapps
½ oz. Stoli Razberi vodka
Splash grenadine

 GINA GEREMIA • DOWNTOWN TAVERNE •
NEW HAVEN, CT

Razzberrita

2 oz. lemon juice or lime juice
1 ¼ oz. raspberry schnapps
¾ oz. tequila

Razzsputin

3 oz. cranberry juice
2 oz. grapefruit juice
1 ½ oz. Stoli Razberi vodka
⅛ oz. lime juice
Slice of lime for garnish

Red Carpet

4 oz. lime juice
2 oz. cranberry juice
2 oz. white rum
2 tbsp. superfine sugar

Red Hot Mama

3 oz. heavy cream or milk
1 oz. Kahlúa
1 oz. Red Hot schnapps or 4 dashes
   Tabasco
 Maraschino cherry for garnish

Red Lion

1 oz. gin
1 oz. Grand Marnier
1 oz. lemon juice
1 oz. orange juice

Regal Fizz

2 oz. brandy
1 oz. Benedictine
Juice of ½ lemon
1 tsp. superfine sugar
Carbonated water or seltzer to fill

Reserve Mai-Tai

3 oz. orange juice
1 oz. orgeat
1 oz. passion fruit juice
1 oz. Whaler's Great white rum
1 oz. Whaler's Rare Reserve dark rum
½ oz. lime juice

Reunion

3 oz. orange juice
½ oz. Romana sambuca
½ oz. strawberry liqueur
½ oz. vodka
6 ripe strawberries

Rhett Butler

1 oz. Cointreau
1 oz. Southern Comfort
¾ oz. Rose's lime juice

Rhum Barbancourt Freeze

½ cup ice
2 oz. orange juice
2 oz. Rhum Barbancourt
1 oz. grapefruit juice
1 oz. triple sec
½ oz. lime juice
 Orange wedge and maraschino cherry for
  garnish

Ricki Martini

2 oz. Passoã
1 ½ oz. Mount Gay rum
¼ oz. lime juice

Ritabu

2 oz. Malibu rum
½ oz. triple sec
¼ oz. fresh lime juice

Roasted Toasted Almond

1 oz. amaretto
1 oz. heavy cream
1 oz. Kahlúa
1 oz. vodka

Roman Cow

1 banana, overripe
1 egg
2 oz. rum
1 oz. lemon or lime juice
1 oz. Romana sambuca

Ron's Special

4 oz. Coco Lopez cream of coconut
½ medium banana
3 pineapple slices with juice
2 oz. dark rum
2 oz. light rum
2 oz. vanilla ice cream
6 maraschino cherries with juice
Maraschino cherry for garnish

Root Beer

2 oz. milk
½ oz. brandy
½ oz. dark crème de cacao
¼ oz. Galliano
Cola to fill

Root Beer Colada

3 oz. Coco Lopez cream of coconut
2 oz. Hiram Walker Old Fashioned root
  beer schnapps

Root Beer Float

2 oz. Hiram Walker Old Fashioned root
  beer schnapps
2 oz. milk or vanilla ice cream, depending
  upon desired thickness

Rooty Tooty

4 oz. orange juice
2 oz. DeKuyper root beer schnapps

Rose Cocktail

1 oz. gin
½ oz. apricot brandy
½ oz. French vermouth
2 tsp. grenadine
1 tsp. lemon juice

Rose in June

1 oz. Chambord
1 oz. gin
Juice of 2 limes (small)
Juice of 1 orange

Rose Petal

2 oz. raspberry sherbet
1 oz. cognac
1 oz. white crème de cacao

Rose's International

1 ½ oz. Midori melon liqueur
¾ oz. pistachio liqueur
¾ oz. Rose's lime juice

Rosemary

1 oz. gin
½ oz. cherry brandy
½ oz. French vermouth

Rum Blossom

1 ½ oz. Appleton rum
1 ½ oz. orange juice
½ oz. lemon juice
½ oz. confectioners' sugar

Rum Cobbler

2 oz. Jamaican rum
1 tsp. Bacardi light rum
1 tsp. pineapple syrup

Rum Collins

½ lemon, peeled
2 oz. Puerto Rican rum
1 tsp. superfine sugar

Rum Cow

2 oz. milk or ice cream, depending upon
    desired thickness
2 oz. rum
1 tsp. Angostura bitters
Maraschino cherry for garnish

Rum Fizz

2 oz. Bacardi light rum
1 oz. lemon juice
1 egg white
1 tbsp. superfine sugar

Rum Pickup

2 oz. milk
2 oz. Puerto Rican rum
Carbonated water or soda to fill

Rum Rita

3 oz. pineapple juice
2 oz. Whaler's Great White rum
1 oz. Cointreau
1 oz. lime juice
½ oz. passion fruit syrup
Coarse sugar for rim
Lime wedge for garnish

Rub lime wedge around rim of glass and dip in coarse sugar.

Rum Runner

1 ½ oz. Bacardi Black rum
1 oz. blackberry brandy
1 oz. crème de banana
½ oz. grenadine
½ oz. lime juice

Rum Yum

1 oz. Baileys Irish cream
1 oz. heavy cream or milk
1 oz. Malibu rum

Rumidori

3 oz. orange or pineapple juice
1 ½ oz. Puerto Rican rum
1 oz. Midori melon liqueur

Russian Funk

3 dashes vodka
Dash lime juice
½ tsp. superfine sugar
Sparkling water to fill

Russian Sombrero

2 oz. light cream
1 ½ oz. Stoli Kafya vodka
1 oz. Baileys Irish cream

Salt Pond

1 ½ oz. Appleton white Jamaican rum
1 oz. lemon or lime juice
½ oz. triple sec

Sambuca Amore

1 oz. Hiram Walker coffee brandy
1 oz. Hiram Walker sambuca

Sambuca Colada

2 oz. Coco Lopez cream of coconut
2 oz. pineapple juice
1 ¼ oz. ice
1 oz. Romana sambuca

Sambuca Satin

3 oz. vanilla ice cream
1 ½ oz. Hiram Walker sambuca
Maraschino cherry for garnish

San Juan

2 oz. light rum
1 ½ oz. grapefruit juice
1 tbsp. Coco Lopez cream of coconut
1 tbsp. fresh lime juice
1 tbsp. brandy for float

Blend everything but brandy. Float brandy on top.

San Juan Cocktail

1 ½ oz. Bacardi light rum
1 oz. grapefruit juice
½ oz. lemon or lime juice
¼ to ½ oz. Coco Lopez cream of coconut
¼ oz. Bacardi 151 rum for float

Blend everything but the Bacardi 151 rum. Float Bacardi 151 rum on top.

San Juan Side Car

1 ½ oz. Bacardi light rum
1 oz. lemon or lime juice
½ oz. white crème de menthe
Coarse sugar for rim
Lime wheel for garnish

Moisten the rim of a cocktail glass and dip in sugar.

San Juan Sling

3 oz. sweetened lemon mix
1 ½ oz. Puerto Rican rum
¾ oz. cherry brandy
½ oz. grenadine for float

Santiago Julep

1 lime, peeled
2 oz. Bacardi light rum
2 tbsp. pineapple juice
2 tsp. grenadine

Blend everything but grenadine. Float grenadine on top.

Sarah Screamer

1 oz. dark rum
1 oz. orange juice
1 oz. pineapple juice
½ oz. citrus vodka
½ oz. peach schnapps
½ oz. sloe gin

Saronnada

2 oz. pineapple juice
1 ½ oz. Disaronno amaretto
1 oz. Coco Lopez cream of coconut
½ oz. vodka

Saronno Fruit Whirl

½ cup canned apricot halves or crushed
   pineapple
1 oz. Disaronno amaretto
1 oz. orange or pineapple yogurt

Sauza La Bamba

1 banana
¾ oz. Frangelico
¾ oz. Sauza Conmemorativo tequila
½ oz. orange juice
7-Up for float

Blend everything but 7-Up. Float 7-Up on top.

Scorpion

2 oz. orange juice
1 oz. light rum
1 oz. sweet and sour mix
½ oz. brandy
½ oz. gin
Dash white crème de menthe
Dash bitters
Orchid for garnish

Scorpion II

2 oz. gold rum
1 ½ oz. fresh lemon juice
1 ½ oz. orange juice
1 oz. brandy
½ oz. orgeat syrup
Orange and lemon slices for garnish

Scotch Smoothie

2 oz. vanilla ice cream
1 ¼ oz. scotch
1 oz. Coco Lopez cream of coconut
½ oz. Baileys Irish cream
½ oz. almond liqueur
Maraschino cherry for garnish

Sea Breeze Margarita

3 oz. grapefruit juice
2 oz. Sauza Conmemorativo tequila
1 oz. cranberry juice
Lime wedges for garnish

Serendipity

2 oz. pineapple juice
1 ½ oz. amaretto
1 ½ oz. Coco Lopez cream of coconut
Maraschino cherry for garnish

Sex in the Blender

2 oz. heavy cream or milk
1 oz. Kahlúa
½ oz. amaretto
2 maraschino cherries for garnish

Shakon Cherry

2 oz. vanilla ice cream
1 oz. Captain Morgan spiced rum
½ oz. maraschino cherry juice
½ oz. wild cherry brandy
Whipped cream and maraschino cherry for
    garnish

 MIKE REAILLY • WATERBURY, VT

Shamrock

1 oz. Irish whiskey
½ oz. dry vermouth
½ oz. green crème de menthe
½ oz. Irish cream

Shark Bite

3 oz. orange juice
2 oz. Myer's Original dark rum
1 oz. grenadine
1 oz. lemon juice

Sharky Highball

2 oz. applejack
½ oz. bourbon
1 tsp. lemon juice
1 tsp. sugar syrup
Carbonated water or soda to fill

Ship's Mate

1 oz. dark Jamaican rum
½ oz. sweet vermouth
½ oz. white crème de cacao
½ oz. white crème de menthe

Sidecar

1 oz. Rémy Martin
½ oz. Cointreau
½ oz. lime juice
1 egg white

Silhouette

4 oz. maraschino cherry juice
4 oz. pineapple juice
1 oz. gin
1 oz. lemon juice
2–3 mint leaves
3–4 pineapple chunks and maraschino
    cherries for garnish

Serve in a margarita glass.

 RONNY HOVANESSIA • GLENDALE, CA

Silk Stocking

3 ½ oz. evaporated milk or 2 oz. vanilla
    ice cream, depending upon desired
    thickness
2 oz. grenadine
2 oz. white tequila
½ oz. crème de cacao
Ground cinnamon for garnish

Silver Fizz

1 ½ oz. gin or rum
Juice ½ lemon
1 egg white
1 tsp. superfine sugar

Slalom

1 oz. Absolut vodka
1 oz. Romana sambuca
1 oz. white crème de cacao
1 tsp. heavy cream

Sloe Tequila

¾ shot tequila
¼ shot sloe gin
Splash lime juice

Slow Boat

2 oz. Appleton gold Jamaican rum
2 oz. grapefruit juice
2 oz. orange juice
½ tsp. superfine sugar
Dash Angostura bitters
Maraschino cherry for garnish

Slow Gin Colada

3 oz. orange juice
2 oz. Coco Lopez cream of coconut
1 oz. light rum
½ oz. gin
½ oz. sloe gin
½ oz. vodka

Smooth as Silk

¾ oz. Irish cream
¾ oz. Vandermint liqueur
½ oz. Copa de Oro coffee liqueur

Smooth Operator

½ banana
1 oz. Frangelico
½ oz. Baileys Irish cream
½ oz. Kahlúa

Smooth Screw

3 oz. pineapple juice
2 oz. Tia Maria
½ oz. Jamaican rum for float

Blend the first two ingredients. Float Jamaican rum on top.

Snow Cap Colada

2 oz. Coco Lopez cream of coconut
1 oz. almond liqueur
1 oz. heavy cream
1 oz. white crème de cacao
½ oz. brandy

Snow Drop

1 oz. light cream
½ oz. Cointreau
½ oz. Galliano
½ oz. vodka
½ oz. white crème de cacao
Dash egg white

Snow Job

2 parts DeKuyper Harvest Pear schnapps
1 part heavy cream or half-and-half

Snowball Colada

4 oz. orange juice
1 oz. Coco Lopez cream of coconut
1 oz. grenadine
1 oz. light rum
1 oz. peach schnapps

Somosa Bay

2 oz. sweet and sour mix
1 oz. Absolut vodka
1 oz. orange juice
½ oz. Grand Marnier
¼ oz. Angostura lime juice

Southern Alexander

2 oz. half-and-half or vanilla ice cream,
    depending upon desired thickness
1 ½ oz. crème de cacao
1 ½ oz. Southern Comfort

Southern Banana Daiquiri

3 oz. Southern Comfort
1 ripe banana, sliced
1 oz. sweetened lime juice

Southern Colada

2 oz. pineapple juice
1 ½ oz. Southern Comfort
1 oz. cream of coconut

Southern Lady

4 oz. grapefruit juice
1 ½ oz. Bacardi light rum
1 egg white
½ oz. grenadine

Southern Smoothie

2 oz. cranberry juice cocktail
1 oz. Coco Lopez cream of coconut
1 oz. Southern Comfort

Southern Stinger

3 oz. white crème de menthe
1 oz. Southern Comfort
Lemon twist for garnish

Southern Strawberry Daiquiri

2 oz. orange juice
1 ½ oz. Southern Comfort
3 strawberries, frozen
Strawberry for garnish

Soviet Cocktail

1 ½ oz. vodka
½ oz. dry sherry
½ oz. dry vermouth
Lemon twist for garnish

Spanish Sparkler

1 cup ice
½ fresh orange, peeled and quartered
2 oz. Madeira wine
2 oz. red sparkling wine
½ oz. rainbow sherbet
Ginger ale to fill
Orange slice and red grapes for garnish

Spearmint Colada

3 oz. Coco Lopez cream of coconut
3 oz. vanilla ice cream
1 ½ oz. Hiram Walker spearmint schnapps
Maraschino cherry and orange slice for
    garnish

Special Sour

1 oz. Grand Marnier
1 oz. lemon juice
1 oz. scotch or bourbon

Spectacular Daiquiri

¾ oz. light rum
¾ oz. Mandarine Napoleon
½ oz. lime juice

Spellbound Shake

3 oz. iced coffee
1 oz. Kahlúa
1 oz. crème de cacao
Heavy cream or milk for float
Mint sprig for garnish

Blend the first three ingredients. Float heavy cream or milk on top and garnish with a fresh mint sprig.

Spiced Piña Colada

3 oz. Coco Lopez piña colada mix
1 oz. Bacardi spiced rum

Spirited Coffee Lopez

6 oz. hot coffee
1 oz. Coco Lopez cream of coconut
½ oz. Irish whiskey
Whipped cream and maraschino cherry for
    garnish

Splendito

2 oz. light rum
3 pineapple chunks, plus 1 for garnish
½ oz. Cointreau
1 tsp. superfine sugar
Maraschino cherry for garnish

Spyglass

2 oz. vanilla ice cream
1 oz. Captain Morgan spiced rum
1 tbsp. honey
Dash milk

St. Patrick's Day Special

1 ½ oz. Bacardi light rum
¾ oz. lemon juice or lime juice
½ oz. green crème de menthe

St. Petersburg Sundae

2 oz. chocolate ice cream
1 ½ oz. Stoli Vanil vodka
½ oz. Disaronno amaretto
Toasted almonds, chopped, for garnish

Standard Flip

2 oz. liquor or wine of your choice
1 whole egg
1 tsp. powdered sugar

Stinger

2 oz. brandy or cognac
½ oz. white crème de menthe

Stralmond Colada

½ cup sliced fresh strawberries
3 oz. pineapple juice
2 oz. Coco Lopez cream of coconut
1 oz. almond liqueur
1 oz. light rum
6 stemless maraschino cherries with juice

Stranded South of France

2 oz. Bartenders Original strawberry tequila
  cream
2 oz. vanilla ice cream
1 oz. Chambord

Straw Hat

1 ½ oz. Puerto Rican rum
1 ½ oz. sweetened lemon mix
½ oz. dark crème de cacao

Strawberry Banana Colada

½ medium banana
2 oz. Coco Lopez cream of coconut
2 oz. strawberries
1 ½ oz. rum

Strawberry Blonde

3 oz. strawberries, fresh or frozen
1 oz. Jose Cuervo tequila
½ oz. Finlandia vodka
½ oz. Grand Marnier
½ oz. pineapple juice

Strawberry Blonde II

½ cup strawberries, fresh or frozen
2 oz. vanilla ice cream
1 oz. Stoli Strasberi vodka
1 oz. white crème de cacao

Strawberry Colada

½ cup strawberries, fresh or frozen
4 oz. pineapple juice
2 oz. rum
1 oz. Coco Lopez cream of coconut

Strawberry Colada II

2 oz. pineapple juice
1 ¼ oz. Leroux strawberry liqueur
1 oz. Coco Lopez cream of coconut

Strawberry Daiquiri

3 oz. Coco Lopez strawberry daiquiri mix
1 oz. Bacardi light rum

Strawberry Daiquiri II

1 10-oz. can Bacardi Frozen Mixers
    Strawberry Daiquiri
3 oz. Bacardi Silver rum

Makes three 8-oz. servings.

Strawberry Daiquiri Alizé

½ cup crushed ice
½ cup frozen strawberries
2 oz. Alizé
1 tbsp. freshly squeezed lemon juice
1 tbsp. superfine sugar

Strawberry Daiquiribe

½ cup fresh strawberries
2 oz. CocoRibe
½ oz. lime juice
½ tsp. superfine sugar

Strawberry Margarita

½ cup strawberries, fresh or frozen
1 oz. tequila
1 oz. Rose's lime juice
½ oz. Cointreau

Strawberry Patch

3 oz. frozen strawberries
2 oz. orange juice
1 ½ oz. Southern Comfort

Strawberry Rose

½ cup strawberries, fresh or frozen
4 oz. rose wine
½ oz. Rose's lime juice
1 tbsp. superfine sugar

Strawberry Shake

½ cup frozen strawberries, slightly thawed
½ cup milk
1 ½ oz. Disaronno amaretto
1 oz. vanilla ice cream

Summer Breeze

2 oz. Coco Lopez cream of coconut
1 ½ oz. Cruzan premium dark rum
1 ½ oz. orange juice
1 ½ oz. pineapple juice

Summer Delight

1 ½ oz. Bacardi light rum
¾ oz. lemon or lime juice
½ tsp. superfine sugar
Dash bitters

Summer Sky Appleton V/X Orange Dalquiri

1 oz. Appleton Estate V/X Jamaican rum
Juice of 1 orange
Juice of ¼ lime
1 tsp. superfine sugar
Sprig of mint and an orange rind for garnish

Summer Squall

1 ½ cups ice
3 oz. cranberry cocktail
3 oz. grapefruit juice
¾ oz. dark rum
½ oz. Captain Morgan coconut rum
¼ oz. Rose's sweetened lime juice
Lime wedge for garnish

Pour into a 16-oz. glass.

Sunshine Colada

1 cup ice
1 ½ oz. orange juice
1 oz. Coco Lopez
¾ oz. brandy
½ oz. Grand Marnier
½ oz. heavy cream

Sunshine Frosty Punch

2 oz. vanilla ice cream
1 ¼ oz. vodka
Maraschino cherry for garnish

Sunshine Surprise

1 cup ice
1 banana, reserving a slice for garnish
2 oz. Coco Lopez cream of coconut
2 oz. simple syrup
2 oz. white Riesling

Sunsplash

5 oz. orange juice
1 ¼ oz. Frangelico
¾ oz. Captain Morgan spiced rum
¾ oz. Coco Lopez cream of coconut

Surf's Up

5 oz. pineapple juice
1 oz. heavy cream
1 oz. rum
½ oz. crème de banana
½ oz. crème de cacao
Three maraschino cherries for garnish

Susquehanna Sunrise

3 oz. cranberry juice
1 ½ oz. wilderberry schnapps
1 oz. grapefruit juice
1 oz. maraschino cherry juice
1 oz. orange juice
1 oz. strawberry daiquiri mix

 LUCIANO MIELE • WILLIAMSPORT, PA

Sweet Almond

1 ½ oz. Disaronno amaretto
1 oz. Coco Lopez cream of coconut
½ oz. heavy cream
½ oz. rum

Sweet Georgia Brown

2 oz. coffee
2 oz. Southern Comfort

Sweet Yello Gal

3 oz. frozen mango
2 oz. Bacardi dark rum
2 oz. Coco Lopez cream of coconut
1 oz. sweetened pineapple juice, frozen
½ oz. simple syrup

Taboo

1 oz. Finlandia vodka, chilled
½ oz. cranberry juice
½ oz. pineapple juice
½ oz. sweet and sour mix
Splash triple sec
Pineapple wedge and maraschino cherry
    for garnish

Tabuka

¼ fresh apple, peeled and cored
2 oz. rum
1 tbsp. lemon juice
1 tbsp. superfine sugar

Tahoe Cocktail

1 ½ oz. Bacardi light rum
¾ oz. lemon juice or lime juice
½ oz. cherry liqueur

Tall Tahoe

1 ½ oz. Bacardi light rum
½ oz. cherry brandy cream
½ oz. light crème de cacao
Maraschino cherry for garnish

Tamara Lvova

1 oz. crème de cacao
1 oz. Rhum Barbancourt
1 oz. Stoli Strasberi vodka
1 oz. vanilla ice cream
Whipped cream and maraschino cherry for
   garnish

Tampa Bay Special

1 ½ oz. Bacardi light rum
¾ oz. orange juice
½ oz. light crème de cacao

Tashkent Cooler

3 oz. freshly squeezed orange juice
1 ½ oz. Stoli Persik vodka
½ oz. sloe gin
Orange slice for garnish

Tennis Love Fizz

2 oz. orange juice
1 ½ oz. Bacardi light rum
1 egg white
Club soda to fill

Tequila Colada

2 ½ oz. Coco Lopez cream of coconut
1 oz. tequila

Tequila Gimlet

1 ½ oz. Rose's lime juice
1 ½ oz. tequila
Lime wheel or green cherry for garnish

Tequilada

4 oz. pineapple juice
2 oz. cream of coconut
2 oz. gold tequila
Slice of fresh pineapple for garnish

Texas Sunday

2 oz. heavy cream
1 ½ oz. Bacardi light rum
½ oz. anisette
½ oz. grenadine

The 5:15 Cocktail

4 oz. heavy cream
2 oz. Curaçao or triple sec
1 oz. French vermouth

The Don Julio Silver Margarita

1 oz. Don Julio silver tequila
1 oz. Rose's lime juice
⅔ oz. orange liqueur

The Flapper

¾ oz. Mandarine Napoleon
¼ oz. triple sec
Orange juice to fill

The Peg Leg

3 oz. apple juice
2 oz. cranberry cocktail
1 oz. Captain Morgan spiced rum
½ oz. Rose's sweetened lime juice
Tall cinnamon stick for garnish

Pour into a 16-oz. glass.

Tia Banana Ria

½ banana
2 oz. Coco Lopez cream of coconut
2 oz. coffee liqueur
2 oz. half-and-half
1 oz. vodka

Tidal Wave

2 oz. orange sherbet
¾ oz. Southern Comfort
¾ oz. vodka
Dash grenadine

Tidal Wave II

2 oz. piña colada mix
2 oz. sweet and sour mix
1 oz. orange juice
¾ oz. Midori melon liqueur
¼ oz. rum
Maraschino cherry for garnish

Tidbit

1 oz. gin
1 oz. vanilla ice cream
1–3 drops dry sherry
Maraschino cherry for garnish

Tiger Tail

4 oz. freshly squeezed orange juice
2 oz. Pernod
¼ tsp. Cointreau
Lime wedge for garnish

Tijuana Margarita

1 ½ oz. sweet and sour mix
1 ½ oz. tequila
1 oz. Hiram Walker Orchard orange
   schnapps

To Die For

1 oz. Godiva liqueur
½ oz. cherry juice
½ oz. cream
¼ oz. Licor 43
Grated nutmeg for garnish
Maraschino cherry for garnish

Pour into a cocktail glass with ice or strain into
a martini glass.

 ROSETTA WARREN • LODI, NJ

To Russia with Love

1 ½ oz. Stoli Vanil vodka
1 oz. cream or half-and-half
½ egg white
½ oz. Coco Lopez cream of coconut
½ oz. maraschino liqueur
Maraschino cherry for garnish

Toasted Almond

2 oz. light cream
1 ½ oz. Lazzaroni amaretto
1 oz. Copa de Oro coffee liqueur

Toasty Almond Colada

2 oz. cream
1 oz. almond liqueur
1 oz. Coco Lopez cream of coconut
1 oz. Kahlúa

Tom Collins Freeze

3 oz. sweet and sour mix
1 ¼ oz. gin
Orange flag for garnish

Top Banana

2 oz. milk or heavy cream
1 ½ oz. Hiram Walker amaretto
1 oz. Hiram Walker crème de banana
Maraschino cherry for garnish

Top Ten

1 ¼ oz. Captain Morgan spiced rum
1 oz. Coco Lopez cream of coconut
1 oz. heavy cream

Trade Winds

2 oz. gold rum
½ oz. Chambord
½ oz. lime juice
2 tsp. sugar syrup

Trail Mix

4 oz. ice cream of your choice
½ oz. Chambord
½ oz. cherry juice
½ oz. Disaronno amaretto
½ oz. Frangelico
½ oz. Peachtree schnapps
Whipped cream and maraschino cherry for
    garnish

 JANET BOGART • MONMOUTH, IL

Tricolor Cocktail

1 cup ice
3 oz. Coco Lopez cream of coconut
2 oz. orange juice
1 slice kiwi fruit, peeled
1 oz. Licor 43
1 oz. melon liqueur
Dash grenadine

Triple Cherry Smash

1 oz. cherry brandy
1 oz. cherry pucker
3 maraschino cherries for garnish

Cut the cherries to fit on the rim of a martini glass.

 STEVEN J. SCALSKY • ALEXANDRIA, VA

Troika

1 oz. Disaronno amaretto
1 oz. Stoli Persik vodka
½ oz. lemon juice
½ oz. sloe gin

Tropical Belle

½ oz. Calvados
½ oz. Galliano
½ oz. gin
1 tsp. maraschino cherry juice
Red and green cherries for garnish

Tropical Blush

3 oz. cranberry juice cocktail
1 oz. Coco Lopez cream of coconut
1 oz. vodka

Tropical Breeze

2 oz. orange juice
1 oz. Coco Lopez cream of coconut
1 oz. rum
½ oz. crème de banana
Pineapple spear and maraschino cherry for
    garnish

Tropical Cocktail

5 oz. pineapple juice
2 oz. grapefruit juice
1 ¼ oz. Myers's rum
Dash grenadine
Fresh orchid and pineapple wedge for garnish

Tropical Cream Punch

3 oz. orange juice
2 oz. Coco Lopez cream of coconut
2 oz. pineapple juice
1 ½ oz. light rum
1 oz. grenadine
Maraschino cherry for garnish

Tropical Freeze

1 ½ oz. orange juice
1 ½ oz. pineapple juice
1 ¼ oz. rum
1 oz. Coco Lopez cream of coconut
½ oz. grenadine
Maraschino cherry for garnish

Tropical Hut

2 oz. Midori melon liqueur
1 ¼ oz. sweet and sour mix
1 oz. rum
¼ oz. orgeat syrup

Tropical Kahlúa

3 oz. Coco Lopez cream of coconut
1 oz. Kahlúa
½ oz. vodka

Tropical Paradise

½ banana
2 oz. Coco Lopez cream of coconut
2 oz. orange juice
1 ¼ oz. rum
¼ oz. grenadine
Maraschino cherry for garnish

Tropical Passion

3 oz. pineapple juice
1 oz. Alizé
1 oz. Midori melon liqueur
1 oz. orange juice
Speared pineapple wedge and maraschino
   cherry for garnish

Tropical Peach

2 oz. orange juice
1 oz. Coco Lopez cream of coconut
1 oz. crème de banana
1 oz. peach schnapps

Tropical Storm

3 oz. orange juice
½ ripe banana, sliced
1 shot dark rum
½ shot crème de banana
Dash grenadine
Maraschino cherry and orange slice for
    garnish

Tropical Treasure

2 oz. Coco Lopez cream of coconut
2 oz. pineapple juice
1 ¼ oz. melon liqueur
1 oz. crème de banana
Maraschino cherry and orange slice for
    garnish

Tumbleweed

2 oz. heavy cream
1 oz. Disaronno amaretto
1 oz. white crème de cacao
Maraschino cherry for garnish

Twist

2 oz. orange sherbet
¾ oz. Absolut vodka
½ oz. Hiram Walker white crème de menthe

Vanil Cocktail

2 oz. orange juice
1 oz. Stoli Vanil vodka
½ oz. Bombay gin
½ oz. triple sec
Maraschino cherry for garnish

Vanilla Sunrise

4 oz. orange juice
1 oz. grenadine
1 oz. Whaler's Vanille rum

Vanya's Strawberry Fizz

6 large strawberries
2 oz. cranberry juice
1 ½ oz. Stoli Strasberi vodka

Velvet Hammer

1 oz. Cointreau
1 oz. heavy cream
1 oz. Kahlúa

Vermillion Twister

¾ oz. brandy
¾ oz. French vermouth
¼ oz. grenadine
3 dashes Curaçao
2 drops Angostura bitters

Very Berry Colada

3 oz. Coco Lopez cream of coconut
2 oz. pineapple juice
1 ½ oz. wildberry schnapps
Maraschino cherry for garnish

Very Cherry Berry

1 ½ oz. Absolut vodka
½ oz. Chambord
½ oz. maraschino cherry juice
4 maraschino cherries

 FRANK DISCIASCIO • SOMERS POINT, NJ

Villa Roma

4 oz. orange juice
1 oz. Galliano
Juice of ¼ lime

 J. GANNON • VILLA ROMA • SAN FRANCISCO, CA

Vodka Collins Freeze

3 oz. sweet and sour mix
1 ¼ oz. vodka
Orange flag for garnish

Vodka Margarita

1 ½ oz. sweet and sour mix
1 ½ oz. vodka
¾ oz. Cointreau
¾ oz. lime juice

Vodka Stone Sour

2 oz. orange juice
1 ½ oz. Gordon's citrus vodka
1 tsp. lemon bar mix
Orange slice and maraschino cherry for
    garnish

Volcano

2 oz. Coco Lopez cream of coconut
1 oz. vanilla ice cream
1 oz. vodka
½ oz. crème de almond
Maraschino cherry for garnish

Volga Cooler

1 oz. crème de banana
1 oz. Stoli Vanil vodka
½ oz. triple sec
Lemon-lime soda to fill
Maraschino cherry for garnish

Wallbanger Freeze

3 oz. orange juice
1 ½ oz. vodka
¼ oz. Galliano for float

Blend the first two ingredients. Float Galliano on top.

Walley's Highball

2 oz. gin
½ oz. Cointreau
½ oz. crème de menthe
Juice of ½ lemon
Carbonated water or soda to fill

Wango Tango

1 ½ oz. Midori melon liqueur
1-2 oz. heavy cream
¾ oz. blue Curaçao
6 pineapple chunks
Maraschino cherry for garnish

Watermelon Rum Runner

1 oz. grenadine
1 oz. Marie Brizard watermelon liqueur
¾ oz. light rum
½ oz. dark rum
½ oz. Marie Brizard blackberry liqueur
½ oz. Marie Brizard crème de banana

Wave Cutter

1 ½ oz. Mount Gay rum
1 oz. orange juice
1 oz. cranberry juice

Wedding Belle

1 oz. cherry brandy
1 oz. Dubonnet
1 oz. gin
1 oz. orange juice

Whale's Breath

1 oz. cranberry juice
1 oz. Whaler's Pineapple Paradise rum
4 oz. orange juice

Whaler's Rum Rita

2 oz. Whaler's Great White rum
1 oz. lime juice
1 oz. triple sec
Coarse salt for rim
Lime wedge for garnish

Whaler's Vanilla Rita

2 oz. Whaler's Vanille rum
1 oz. orange juice
1 oz. triple sec
½ oz. lime juice
Orange wedge for garnish

Whisper Cocktail

½ oz. whiskey
½ oz. French vermouth
½ oz. Italian vermouth

White Cap

1 ½ oz. crème de cacao
1 ½ oz. Southern Comfort
1 oz. half-and-half

White Gorilla

2 oz. DeKuyper root beer schnapps
1 ½ oz. Gilbey's vodka
½ oz. milk

White Lily

2 oz. gin
1 ½ oz. light rum
1 ½ oz. triple sec
¼ tsp. Pernod

White Mink

2 oz. Galliano
1 oz. Rémy Martin cognac
1 oz. vanilla ice cream
1 oz. white crème de cacao

White Plush Highball

4 oz. milk
1 ½ oz. gin
1 oz. maraschino liqueur

White Russian

1 ½ oz. vodka
½ oz. Kahlúa
½ oz. vanilla ice cream

White Tiger

2 oz. vanilla ice cream
1 oz. Tuaca
½ oz. white crème de cacao
Maraschino cherry for garnish

White Velvet

1 ½ oz. Romana sambuca
1 egg white
1 oz. lemon juice

Who's Your Daddy

2 oz. Dad's root beer
1 ½ oz. Bartenders Hot Sex
1 oz. Captain Morgan spiced rum

 TIM LOWERY • WI

Wildberry Angel

16 oz. strawberry-flavored water
1 12-oz. can frozen pink lemonade
3 oz. Gordon's wildberry vodka
1 ½ oz. crème de cassis
Strawberry for garnish

Willawa

2 oz. cream
1 oz. Galliano
½ oz. cherry brandy
½ oz. Rémy Martin cognac
Grated nutmeg for garnish

Winter Frost

3 oz. vanilla ice cream
1 oz. brandy
½ oz. white crème de cacao
½ oz. white crème de menthe
Maraschino cherry for garnish

Winter in the Emerald Isle

3 oz. vanilla ice cream
1 oz. green crème de menthe
1 oz. Irish whiskey

Winter Orange Blossom

3 oz. orange juice
1 oz. gin
½ tsp. superfine sugar

Wynbreezer

2 oz. orange juice
1 oz. Angostura lime juice
1 oz. dark rum
1 oz. triple sec

Yacht Club Fizz

2 oz. pineapple juice
1 ½ oz. Bacardi light rum
1 egg white
Club soda to fill

Pineapple spear and maraschino cherry for garnish

Zombie

2 ½ oz. light rum
1 oz. dark rum
1 oz. orange juice
1 oz. pineapple juice
1 oz. triple sec
½ oz. Angostura grenadine
½ oz. apricot brandy

All cocktails should be blended with ice.

Apple Berry Jive

6 oz. apple juice
2 oz. frozen raspberries, thawed
2 oz. vanilla ice cream
Apple slice for garnish

Apple Strawberry Surprise

2 ½ cups apple juice
1 cup frozen strawberries, thawed
½ tsp. superfine sugar
Canada Dry ginger ale, chilled, to fill
Fresh strawberries for garnish

Makes 4 servings.

Appleberry Freeze

5 oz. apple juice
1 oz. strawberries in syrup
Fresh strawberry for garnish

Banana Lopez

1 medium banana
2 oz. Coco Lopez cream of coconut
1 tsp. lemon juice

Banana Smoothie

1 cup yogurt, plain or flavored
1 ripe banana cut into pieces
2 tbsp. honey, or to taste, if desired
½ tsp. vanilla

Berry Surprise

1 cup frozen raspberries, thawed
½ tsp. superfine sugar
2 ½ cups apple juice
Canada Dry ginger ale, chilled, to fill
Fresh raspberries for garnish

Makes 4 servings.

Bite of the Apple

5 oz. apple juice
1 oz. fresh lime juice
1 tbsp. unsweetened applesauce
Ground cinnamon for garnish

Blue Fruit Ice

5 oz. grapefruit juice
1 oz. frozen blueberries, thawed
½ oz. Rose's grenadine syrup

Blueberry Shake

1 cup milk
½ cup fresh blueberries
1 tbsp. superfine sugar
Fresh blueberries or strawberries for garnish

Blushing Bride

4 oz. orange juice
3 oz. pink grapefruit juice
1 oz. Coco Lopez cream of coconut
½ oz. grenadine

Bodacious Freeze

6 oz. cranberry cocktail
½ cup peaches in heavy syrup
¼ oz. Rose's grenadine syrup
Lemon wheel for garnish

Chiquitita

1 banana
2 oz. pineapple juice
1 oz. grenadine
1 oz. light cream
Orange slice or paper umbrella for garnish

Chocolate Banana Colada Shake

1 ½ cups chocolate or vanilla ice cream
½ cup milk
½ cup sliced banana
⅓ cup Coco Lopez cream of coconut
1 tbsp. chocolate syrup

Chocolate Colada Shake

½ cup chocolate or vanilla ice cream
½ cup milk
⅓ cup Coco Lopez cream of coconut
1 tbsp. chocolate syrup
Maraschino cherry for garnish

Chocolate Malted Milk

½ pint milk
2 oz. syrup
1 oz. chocolate ice cream
1 tsp. powdered, unflavored malt

Blend on high speed for about 1 ½ minutes, or until mixture is thick and there is about twice the original amount. Serve in two soda glasses.

Makes 2 servings.

Clown Noses

3 oz. orange juice
⅓ cup maraschino cherries, stemless
Splash Rose's grenadine syrup for float
Orange wheel for garnish

Combine the juice and ice in a blender until smooth. Add the cherries and blend very briefly (large chunks of cherry should be visible). Top with grenadine and garnish with an orange wheel.

Coco Lopez Shake

2 ½ oz. Coco Lopez cream of coconut
1 oz. vanilla ice cream
Maraschino cherry for garnish

Coco Mocha Lopez

4 oz. Coco Lopez cream of coconut
2 oz. cold, black coffee
½ tsp. brandy
Grated nutmeg for garnish

Coconut/Cranberry Smoothie

8 oz. cranberry juice
3 oz. Angostura lime juice
3 oz. Coco Lopez cream of coconut

Crananna Chill

6 oz. cranberry cocktail
½ banana
Dash of lemon juice
Lemon wedge for garnish

Cranapple Slush

3 oz. apple juice
2 oz. cranberry cocktail
1 oz. Mr & Mrs T sweet and sour mix
½ oz. Rose's grenadine
Lemon wheel for garnish

Cranberry Cappuccino

7 oz. cranberry cocktail
1 oz. half-and-half
¾ oz. cold espresso
½ oz. hazelnut syrup
Ground cinnamon for garnish

Cranberry Dew

6 oz. cranberry cocktail
2 oz. honeydew melon puree
¼ oz. Rose's lime juice
Lime wheel for garnish

Cranberry Mint Freeze

6 oz. cranberry cocktail
3 After Eight dark chocolate thin mints,
    plus 1 for garnish
1 oz. vanilla ice cream
Whipped cream for garnish

Cranberry Smoothie

6 oz. cranberry cocktail
½ Granny Smith apple, seeded
¾ oz. raspberry syrup
Apple slice for garnish

Deep Freeze

½ cup ice
4 oz. apple juice
1 oz. ginger ale or Sprite to fill
1 oz. peach nectar
Lemon wheel for garnish

Dreamsicle

4 oz. orange juice
3 oz. peach nectar
2 oz. half-and-half
¾ oz. almond syrup
Peach slice and whipped cream for garnish

Floribbean Freeze

3 oz. cranberry cocktail juice
3 oz. grapefruit juice
2 oz. vanilla ice cream
1 tsp. Coco Lopez cream of coconut
Orange wedge for garnish

Florida Banana Lopez

4 oz. orange juice
1 medium banana
2 oz. Coco Lopez cream of coconut

Frozen Apricot Orange Lopez

2 oz. apricot nectar
2 oz. Coco Lopez cream of coconut
1 ½ oz. orange juice

Frozen Citrus Mary

5 oz. orange juice
4 oz. tomato juice
¼ oz. Rose's sweetened lime juice
½ tsp. prepared horseradish
6 drops Worcestershire sauce
Orange wheel for garnish

Frozen Cranberry Cappuccino

6 oz. cranberry cocktail
1 oz. vanilla ice cream
¾ oz. cold espresso
Ground cinnamon for garnish

Frozen Lime Soda

6 oz. Canada Dry club soda
6 oz. cold water
1 6-oz. can frozen limeade concentrate,
    slightly thawed
1 6-oz. can frozen pineapple juice,
    slightly thawed
6 lime slices and 6 maraschino cherries for
    garnish

Makes 6 servings.

Frozen Orange Mochaccino

5 oz. orange juice
1 oz. cold espresso
1 tbsp. chocolate syrup
Orange wedge for garnish

Gin-Less Gimlet

Juice of ½ lime
1 egg white
2 tsp. sugar syrup (or to taste)
2 dashes Angostura bitters

Grape Lopez

4 oz. grape juice
3 oz. Coco Lopez cream of coconut

Ground Pterodactyl Eyes

½ cup seedless red grapes
3 oz. grapefruit juice
¾ oz. Mr & Mrs T piña colada mix

Combine the juice, colada mix, and ice in a blender until smooth. Add the grapes and blend briefly (leaving large chunks). Serve with a spoon.

Guacamole Cocktail

1 California avocado, peeled and diced
5 oz. tomato juice, chilled
2 oz. fresh lime juice, chilled
1 small green chile, chopped
1 garlic clove, minced
Salt to taste
Freshly ground black pepper to taste
Lime wedge for garnish

Jungle Punch

6 oz. apple juice
½ banana
1 oz. canned mandarin oranges
   (or 1 oz. orange juice)
Orange wedge for garnish

Lime Sorbet Lopez

2 ½ oz. Coco Lopez cream of coconut
1 oz. lime sherbet
½ oz. Major Peters' lime juice

Major Peters' Frozen Virgin Mary

5 oz. orange juice
4 oz. Major Peters' bloody mary mix
  (regular or hot & spicy)
¼ oz. Major Peters' lime juice

Maui Squeeze

6 oz. orange juice
¼ cup canned pineapple cubes (packed
  in juice)
½ oz. Mr & Mrs T piña colada mix
Orange or pineapple wedge for garnish

Melon Medley

4 oz. cantaloupe, cubed
4 oz. fresh orange juice
½ oz. fresh lemon juice

Mocho Joe Cooler

4 oz. brewed coffee
4 oz. evaporated milk or half-and-half
4 oz. mocha powder
Whipped cream and maraschino cherry for
  garnish

Mocquiri

3 oz. pineapple juice
½ tsp. lemon juice
½ tsp. Rose's lime juice
1 tsp. confectioners' sugar
Lime slice for garnish

For a Mockardi, or mock Bacardi, add ½ oz. grenadine before blending.

Monterey Madness

6 oz. grapefruit juice
3 oz. cantaloupe puree
¼ oz. Rose's lime juice
1 tsp. superfine sugar
Lime wedge for garnish

Morning

3 oz. tomato juice
1 egg
½ tsp. horseradish
½ tsp. lemon juice
Celery salt for garnish

Mountain Dew

6 oz. apple juice
3 oz. honeydew melon puree
Dash of lemon juice
Lemon wheel for garnish

Nada Colada

2 oz. pineapple juice
1 oz. Coco Lopez cream of coconut

New Orleans Day

2 oz. Coco Lopez cream of coconut
1 oz. butterscotch topping
1 oz. half-and-half

Nor'easter Surprise

5 oz. grapefruit juice
2 oz. tomato juice
⅓ oz. Rose's sweetened lime juice
Lime wedge for garnish

Orange Dream Milkshake

2 oz. vanilla ice cream
1 oz. milk
1 oz. orange juice
Whipped cream and maraschino cherry for
garnish

Orange Fiesta

½ cup orange juice, chilled
¼ cup orange sherbet
¼ cup vanilla ice cream
Orange slice and mint leaf for garnish

Orange Smoothie

3 oz. orange juice
2 ½ oz. Coco Lopez cream of coconut
1 oz. vanilla ice cream
Grated nutmeg for garnish

Orange Sorbet Lopez

2 oz. Coco Lopez cream of coconut
1 oz. orange juice
1 oz. orange sherbet

Orchard Freeze

5 oz. orange juice
½ Granny Smith apple, seeded
¼ oz. Rose's sweetened lime juice
Orange wedge for garnish

Peach Blend

2 cups ice
2 cups milk
1 cup canned peaches
1 banana, sliced
1 tsp. superfine sugar
Maraschino cherries for garnish

Serve immediately in a frosty mug.

Makes 2 servings.

Peach Freeze

5 oz. orange juice
2 oz. peach nectar
¾ oz. raspberry syrup
Orange or peach slice for garnish

Piña Colada Shake

½ cup pineapple juice, unsweetened
⅓ cup Coco Lopez cream of coconut

Pineapple Lopez

½ banana
2 oz. Coco Lopez cream of coconut
1 ½ oz. pineapple juice

Pineapple Sorbet Lopez

2 oz. pineapple juice
1 ½ oz. Coco Lopez cream of coconut
1 oz. pineapple sherbet

Pink Grapefruit Passion

5 oz. grapefruit juice
½ oz. Mr & Mrs T piña colada mix
2 oz. frozen raspberries
Lime wedge for garnish

Pink Sands

3 oz. pineapple juice
2 tbsp. cream
½ tsp. superfine sugar
Dash grenadine

Polynesian Pleasure

2 oz. orange juice
1 oz. pineapple juice
Dash lemon juice

Rainbow Berry Smoothie

½ banana
2 oz. apple or cranberry juice
2 oz. rainbow sherbet
2 oz. whole strawberries, frozen
1 oz. whole blackberries, frozen

Raspberry Chill

1 cup crushed ice
1 cup fresh or frozen raspberries
½ cup nonalcoholic rosé wine
½ cup sour cream
2 oz. Canada Dry ginger ale
Fresh raspberries for garnish

Blend first four ingredients. Just before serving, add Canada Dry ginger ale and stir. Serve in chilled wine glasses.

Makes 8 servings.

Rose's Banana

½ large, ripe banana
1 oz. Rose's lime juice
1 tbsp. confectioners' sugar
Lime slice for garnish

Strawberries and Cream Smoothie

4 oz. Mr & Mrs T strawberry daiquiri mix
4 oz. vanilla ice cream
Whipped cream for garnish

Serve in a 10-oz. mug garnished with whipped cream.

Strawberry Banana Lopez

½ medium banana
2 oz. Coco Lopez cream of coconut
2 oz. strawberries

Strawberry Yogurt Punch

4 oz. orange juice
2 oz. vanilla yogurt
1 oz. strawberries in syrup
Fresh strawberry for garnish

Tangerine Squeeze

6 oz. orange juice
¼ cup canned mandarin oranges
¼ oz. Rose's grenadine syrup
Orange wedge or kiwi wedge for garnish

The Apple Shadow

5 ½ oz. apple juice
½ oz. Mr & Mrs T piña colada mix
Lime wedge for garnish

Tiger's Milk

¾ cup orange juice
¾ cup plain yogurt
1 banana, sliced
2 tsp. honey

Makes 2 servings.

Tropical Breeze

½ banana, sliced
½ cup milk
2 tbsp. pineapple juice
1 tsp. Coco Lopez cream of coconut

Tropical Freeze Lopez

2 oz. Coco Lopez cream of coconut
1 ½ oz. orange juice
1 ½ oz. pineapple juice

Wacky Jamaican Cabdriver

1 oz. Coco Lopez cream of coconut
1 oz. cranberry juice
1 oz. orange juice

Well Red Rhino

1 ½ oz. strawberry daiquiri mix
1 oz. cranberry juice cocktail
½ oz. Coco Lopez cream of coconut
Club soda to fill

Blend the first three ingredients. Add club soda
to the top and stir.

Worms and Dirt

4 oz. apple juice
1 oz. vanilla ice cream
1 Oreo chocolate sandwich cookie
Gummy worm for garnish

YOUR BLENDER RECIPES

DRINK INDEX

B

305

313

T

Y

Z

ALCOHOL INDEX

Ray Foley, a former marine with more than thirty years of bartending and restaurant experience, is the founder and editor of *Bartender Magazine*. Ray is referred to as "The Legend" for all he has done for bartenders and bartending. *Bartender Magazine* is the only magazine in the world specifically geared toward bartenders and is one of the very few primarily designed for servers of alcohol. *Bartender Magazine* is enjoying its thirty-second year and currently has a steadily growing circulation of more than one hundred thousand.

After serving in the United States Marine Corps and attending Seton Hall University, Ray entered the restaurant business as a bartender, which eventually led to a job as the assistant general manager of The Manor in West Orange, New Jersey, with more than 350 employees.

In 1983, Ray left The Manor to devote his full efforts to *Bartender Magazine*. The circulation and exposure has grown from seven thousand to more than one hundred thousand to date and has become the largest on-premise liquor magazine in the country.

Ray has been published in numerous articles throughout the country and has appeared on many TV and radio shows.

He is the founder of the Bartender Hall of Fame, which honors the best bartenders throughout the United States, not only for their abilities at bartending but for their involvement and service in their communities as well.

Ray is also the founder of The Bartenders' Foundation Incorporated. This nonprofit foundation has been set up to raise scholarship money for bartenders and their families. Scholarships awarded to bartenders can be used to either further their education or can go toward the education of their children.

Ray is the founder of www.bartender.com (more than 1.5 million hits per month), www.USBartender.com, and many other bar-related websites.

Mr. Foley serves as a consultant to some of our nation's foremost distillers and importers. He is also responsible for creating and naming new drinks for the liquor industry. Here are just a few:

"The Fuzzy Navel"
"The Royal Stretch"—for Grand Royal Oaks Race
"The Royal Turf"—for Grand Royal Oaks Race
"Pink Cadillac"
"Pear-A-Terre"
"Grapeful Red"

"Pear A Mud"
"Pearsian Kat"
"Pomtree Cocktail"
"The Royal Sour"
"The Hamptons"
"Golden Apfel"
"Mosquito Bite"

Ray has one of the largest collections of cocktail recipe books in the world, dating back to the 1800s, and is one of the foremost collectors of cocktail shakers, having 368 shakers in his collection.

He is the author of the following best sellers:

Bartending for Dummies
Running a Bar for Dummies
The Ultimate Little Cocktail Book
The Ultimate Little Shooter Book
The Ultimate Little Martini Book
Advice from Anonymous
The Best Irish Drinks
Jokes, Quotes, and Bartoons
Beer is the Answer...What is the Question?
X-Rated Drinks
Bartender Magazine's Ultimate Bartender's Guide
Vodka 1000
Rum 1000
Tequila 1000
The Best Summer Drinks
God Loves Golfers Best

Ray resides in New Jersey with his wife and partner of twenty-nine years, Jackie, and their son, Ryan.

For additional information or a media kit, please contact:

Jaclyn Foley, Publisher
Bartender Magazine
Foley Publishing Corporation
PO Box 158, Liberty Corner, NJ 07938
Telephone: (908) 766-6006
Fax: (908) 766-6607
Email: BarMag@aol.com
Website: www.Bartender.com